American Rye

American Rye

A Guide to the Nation's Original Spirit

Clay Risen

Scott & Nix, Inc.

NEW YORK

ISBN 978-1-935622-75-8

Published by
Scott & Nix, Inc.
150 West 28th Street, Suite 1900
New York, NY 10001
www.scottandnix.com
rye@scottandnix.com

Scott & Nix, Inc. books are distributed to the trade by
Independent Publishers Group (IPG)
814 North Franklin Street
Chicago, IL 60610
800-888-4741
ipgbook.com

Manufactured in South Korea

10 9 8 7 6 5 4 3 2 1

scottandnix.com

Contents

Introduction

My grandmother's dining room was filled with knickknacks: souvenir spoons and matchbook covers and whimsical porcelains. She collected toothpick holders and kept them in a tall, wood-paneled vitrine. Everything felt out of time, ephemera from an unspecified past. On a sideboard table stood three glass decanters, and around each of them hung a metal name plate, strung on a loose chain. "Scotch," "Bourbon," and "Rye," they read. Even as a boy, I knew what scotch and bourbon were. Both were, like the spoons and porcelains, anachronisms: Only old men drank scotch, and only hillbillies drank bourbon.

Rye, though, was something else, something paleontological, identifiable by a few elusive traces, like a dinosaur that left just a single footprint by which to remember it. I only knew rye from Don McLean's song "American Pie," with its refrain:

So bye-bye, Miss American Pie
Drove my Chevy to the levee, but the levee was dry
And them good old boys were drinkin' whiskey 'n rye
Singin', "This'll be the day that I die"
"This'll be the day that I die"

At least I could claim youthful ignorance. By then, in the early 1990s, no one else knew much about rye either. It had simply vanished.

What is even more astounding about rye's complete disappearance from the cultural landscape is how much of that territory it once occupied. Bourbon may be America's native spirit, but rye was there first. Almost 150 years before people were mashing, distilling, and aging corn and other grains (including rye) to create bourbon, they were distilling whiskey. It came over with the earliest German immigrants, and with early English settlers who had picked up a taste for the grain from the Germans and Dutch who passed through their island, fleeing constant war on the continent.

Rye is hardy, and it grows like a weed. To some farmers, it was little more than that; at best it was a convenient ground cover to plant among more desirable crops. But it can be easily ground into flour for bread, or brewed to make beer, or distilled to make a spirit. By the eighteenth century rye distilling was common up and down the East Coast. Its production centered in the Hudson Valley and interior of Pennsylvania but could be found from Massachusetts to Virginia, where George Washington, needing a source of income after his presidency, started a rye distillery at Mount Vernon.

Even as the Ohio River Valley boomed and with it the Midwestern whiskey industry (of which bourbon was just one small part), rye distillation held steady in the East. Styles emerged: Pennsylvania rye was often called "Old Monongahela," with a spiciness derived from a high-rye, no-corn mash bill; Maryland rye was known for its sweetness, derived both from its relatively high corn content and from the frequent addition of fruit flavorings. Even Kentucky, the birthplace and home base of bourbon, made its share of rye, though unsurprisingly it relied heavily on corn, which grew in abundance across the Ohio River Valley.

Whiskey fans often speak about the "bourbon bust," the stretch of decades between the 1970s and the end of the 1990s when demand for the spirit cratered. For rye, the entire century was a bust. Prohibition, in the 1920s, had disrupted all manner of American alcohol traditions, but it dealt a near-fatal blow to rye whiskey. Once a workhorse component in a long list of cocktail lounge favorites, rye was practically forgotten by a country that by World War II was growing used to smoother spirits like gin and blended whiskey. Regional rye styles were erased as massive multinational companies bought up distilleries and brands, and, even after Prohibition ended, centralized production in a few Midwestern locations, and in a few homogenized recipes.

After that, what passed as rye was, for the most part, a shade of its former self. Aside from a few Eastern holdouts, most rye was made in the Kentucky style, with almost as much corn as rye in the mash bill. And there wasn't much of it—most distilleries spent just a single day distilling their entire year's quota of rye whiskey. When people did ask for rye, they usually meant Canadian whisky—which, although it's known colloquially as rye, is by American standards something else entirely (we'll get to that).

Mike Swanson, the co-founder of Minnesota's Far North Spirits, recalled the utter lack of awareness about rye among visitors to his distillery. "They said maybe their grandpa drank it, but they hadn't, because it had almost disappeared entirely," he said. "There was probably Old Overholt on the shelf and that was about it."

And then, around 2010, something began to shift. The cocktail renaissance elicited a renewed interest in the bespoke recipes of yesteryear, especially from before Prohibition—recipes that often called for rye. And, as bartenders realized, not just any rye, and certainly not the "rye in name only" being made by Kentucky distilleries, but a robust, spicy, high-rye content rye whiskey. Consumers asked for it too. Food writers refer to the early twenty-first century as a "return to flavor," as Americans set aside preferences for lighter textures and palates in favor of spice, smoke, heat, and earthiness, the sort of characteristics that define rye whiskey. Americans embraced authenticity too. People wanted the things they consumed to do more—they wanted a story, a set of values, an identity, a realness. And what has a better story than rye?

It is not an easy grain to work with; it gums up readily. But therein lies the challenge that many distillers decided to embrace. Bourbon is a delicious whiskey, but its range of possible flavors is limited, and it takes several years of aging for them to bloom. Young rye, in contrast, is beautiful, full of herbaceous, floral, earthy notes, like sticking your head in an herb patch. As rye ages, it takes on depth. Thyme and lavender become mint and chocolate. It incorporates barrel notes but also transforms them; there's the usual caramel and baking spices, but also mole and dried flowers. And as several distillers in this book have shown, rye is a perfect spirit to finish in a wine cask or other used barrel—it takes on port, Sauternes, or rum not to cover existing flavors, but to complement them.

"One thing about corn is that it doesn't have its own flavor," Swanson said. "It allows the barrel flavor to come through. And it just has sweetness, whereas rye has a very distinctive flavor on its own."

Distillers are only beginning to understand the vast breadth of what rye can do, and what they can do with it. Some of them still buy rye whiskey from large distilleries like MGP in Indiana and Alberta Distillers in Canada, then blend the barrels to their preferred flavor profiles. But more are taking on the spirit from scratch, creating whiskeys that not only stand out in their uniqueness, but also stand in for emerging regional styles. We can once again speak of Pennsylvania rye, or Maryland rye, or even New York Empire rye. Distillers are embracing those time-tested styles not as straitjackets, but as starting points. Where they go next, nobody quite yet knows. The return of rye whiskey, and its bright future, are the most exciting, and delicious, stories in American spirits today.

Rye Whiskey, Explained

So what is rye, anyway? As I hope is obvious by now, and contrary to Mr. McLean's song, rye is a type of whiskey, just like bourbon and single malt scotch are types of whiskey. Under federal law (yes, federal law), rye whiskey has to be made from a mash bill, or mix of grains, that contains at least 51 percent rye. The rest can be any other type of grain, be it corn, wheat, barley, rice, triticale, spelt, whatever—though in practice it's usually corn and malted barley. Otherwise, rye whiskey follows the same rules as bourbon, or almost any other kind of whiskey made in the United States, especially in that it has to be aged in new, charred oak barrels.

The malted barley in the mash bill is important, because the malting process—in which grain begins to germinate before being cut off by heating in a kiln—generates enzymes that help jump-start the fermentation process. We'll get to fermentation later, but for now, just remember that these days the malted barley is almost always there for function, not flavor. Traditionally, and especially in Pennsylvania rye traditions, distillers often used malted rye instead of malted barley, and in large enough amounts that it affected the actual flavor of the spirit, lending it a smoother, more refined profile. Recently there has been a resurgence in the use of malted rye, not just in Pennsylvania but even in Kentucky, where New Riff, a distillery across the Ohio River from Cincinnati, employs it to great effect.

There are, historically, three primary styles of American rye whiskey. Pennsylvania rye, often known as Old Monongahela, developed in the western part of the state. The style, which almost completely vanished during Prohibition and was last made in the 1960s, consisted of a mash bill of malted and unmalted rye, fermented as a sweet mash, distilled on a three-chamber still, and aged in heated warehouses. (Again, we'll get to the details about mashes, stills, and warehouses later.) It often contained wheat too; only in southeast Pennsylvania, where corn was (and remains) plentiful, did distillers work with that grain as well.

As a style, Pennsylvania rye was fairly well documented, and since it was still being made until somewhat recently, it has been relatively easy for contemporary distilleries like Dad's Hat, Stoll & Wolfe, and Liberty Pole to resurrect it. It's not as easy with the second style, Maryland rye. That style remains a confounding mystery: It was at one point one of the most widely consumed types of whiskey in America, yet what actually defined it has been forgotten. In a sense distillers have to reverse-engineer Maryland whiskey from the terms used to promote it. We know it was considered sweeter than Old Monongahela. It was almost certainly made with some quantity of corn, but it was also likely, sometimes, mixed with a small amount of fruit juice to give it an extra dollop of sweetness. Indeed, where Old Monongahela was defined prescriptively—by its recipe and its production methods—Maryland rye appears to have been defined descriptively, by its resulting flavor profile. It was sweeter, and whatever it took to get there was considered fair game.

There's another difference between the two: While Old Monongahela was, as far as we know, made exclusively in Pennsylvania, Maryland rye was made not just in Maryland but in states up and down the Eastern Seaboard. Producers in New York and Boston all made "Maryland-style" rye, an indicator to buyers that the whiskey would be sweeter and less spicy than its Pennsylvania cousin. Interestingly, the same thing is true today: New England Distilling, based in Portland, Maine, and Leopold Bros. in Denver, Colorado, have both made a Maryland-style rye whiskey.

The third style is Kentucky rye, made with almost as much corn as rye, with about 5 percent malted barley tossed in. The lower Ohio River Valley is not, historically, a rye-growing region, and as Kentucky took off as the dominant whiskey state after Prohibition, its flagship product, bourbon, demanded almost all its production capacity. But the handful of mega-corporations that had swallowed up distilleries left and right during Prohibition, including most of the distilleries

The four primary rye whiskey styles: Old Monongahela (Dad's Hat), Maryland (Baltimore Spirits Co.), Kentucky (Knob Creek), MGP (Bulleit). MGP isn't an official style, but its 95/5 rye/malted barley mashbill is used by many non-distilling producers, and is so popular that many distillers have copied it.

in Maryland and Pennsylvania, had at least some incentive to continue making something they could call rye whiskey, to satisfy the remaining fans of those now-lost spirits. And so Jim Beam, Heaven Hill, and others did the bare minimum, making whiskey with the minimally permitted amount of rye, for a few days a year, or even just a single day a year.

None of this is meant to put down the Kentucky style. It is essentially a spicy bourbon, made like a bourbon, so that the fresh, zesty herbal notes found in Old Monongahela are harmonized with the sweetness of the corn and, even more, the wood notes coming from the barrel. For decades, this was what people meant when they talked about rye, and even today it's what many continue to expect.

"As a nation, we had evolved from a home of thousands of regional distillers to a very boring and consolidated spirits landscape," said Meredith Meyer Grelli, the co-founder of Pittsburgh's Wigle Whiskey.

There is a fourth rye whiskey style, not historical but of recent origin. It originated at single distillery, the MGP facility in Lawrenceburg, Indiana (renamed Ross & Squib in 2021). Almost all the whiskey it produces it sells to private-label clients, so that its products end up being known by many names: In the case of rye, they include Bulleit, Templeton, Smooth Ambler, and Angel's Envy. The distillery makes different mash bills, but one in particular—95 percent unmalted rye, 5 percent malted barley—has become the consumer favorite for its bold, spicy palate. So dominant has MGP's 95-5 mash bill become that several distilleries making their own whiskey use the same mash bill, knowing its track record with drinkers.

What About Canadian Rye?

Canadian whisky is often called rye, and in Canada "rye" and "whisky" are often synonymous. But it's nothing like American rye. Canadian whisky is made in an entirely different process from American whiskey. In the United States, distilleries mix their grains together into a mash bill, then ferment, distill, and age them as a single batch. Not so in Canada. There, each grain is processed separately, then blended together in the end. Typically, those blends consist of a lightly flavored base spirit, usually made from corn, and a dense, more robust rye for flavor. A little goes a long way: Distillers might use less than 10 percent rye whiskey in their blends. (They can also add small amounts of flavorings or other spirits, or even wine, all of which is forbidden for straight whiskey in the United States.)

Canadian rye is delicious, even if it is a world away from its robust American cousin. And though you might not guess from the huge volumes of Canadian whisky sold in the United States, it actually faces a huge disadvantage. Because its constituent parts are blended after they are aged, and because a majority of it is light whisky, American liquor regulations require it to be labeled a blend, a term that many American consumers associate with bottom-shelf swill. While some Canadian whisky does indeed qualify as swill, much of it is sublime, nuanced, and delicious. You just wouldn't know it from the scarlet B that adorns its label.

Yet here too, things are starting to change. Alberta Distillers, owned by Beam Suntory, has historically made a whisky exclusively with rye grain, which early in the American whiskey renaissance showed up in high-priced brands like WhistlePig, Masterson's, and Lock, Stock & Barrel. It is finally appearing in American markets under its own name. Caribou Crossing, a brand of Canadian whisky owned by Sazerac, is likewise a "high-rye" rye, breaking with Canadian convention but hewing to the new expectations of American whiskey consumers. Although both are outside the scope of this book, they are worth seeking out.

The Global Scene

Rye is no longer an exclusively American, or Canadian, spirit. Several distilleries in Europe, including in Denmark, Germany, and even Scotland, are starting to make it as well. That makes sense: Rye grain came to North America from northern Europe, where it has been a staple of food, beer, and distilling for centuries. Korn, a traditional spirit in Germany and Poland, is made from rye; several vodka companies use rye as well. Again, these whiskeys fall outside the scope of this book. But Stauning, from Denmark, makes a stellar rye, as do Zuidam, from the Netherlands, and Arbikie from Scotland.

But Wait, There's More

Rye whiskey isn't just about the mash bill. To qualify as such in the United States, it has to meet several more standards: It must be distilled to no more than 80 percent alcohol by volume, and it has to go into the barrels at no more than 62.5 percent alcohol. Those barrels, in turn, must be new, they must be made from oak, and they must be charred on the inside. Unlike scotch or Canadian whisky, which must be aged for at least three years, there is no minimum on aging American rye; a distiller can dump it into a barrel and immediately dump it back out and call it rye whiskey.

But there's a catch, in that the barrels, again, must be new, and barrels costs hundreds of dollars. So distillers have an incentive to get as much out of each barrel as they can. Many of those used barrels, by the way, get shipped to Scotland and Mexico, where scotch and tequila makers love them; called ex-bourbon barrels at this point, they have been stripped of their aggressive woodiness and impart softer, more subtle notes. In another sign of rye's global resurgence, in 2018 Glenmorangie, the Highland scotch distillery, released Spìos, a single malt whisky finished in ex-rye casks.

Mixed or Neat?

A major driver in the resurgence of rye whiskey is the cocktail scene. Rye's spiciness makes it a versatile element in a mixed drink, and it's hard to go wrong with a Rye Old Fashioned. But there is also a case for drinking rye neat. Again, one of the wonderful aspects of rye is its diversity: A young rye is earthy and herbaceous, while an older rye is all about chocolate and dried spices, a range that invites uncompromised contemplation. And for those averse to spice, keep in mind that rye is not especially hot, despite its shorthand descriptors—think cinnamon and green pepper, rather than jalapeños.

If you've flipped through this book already, you'll have noticed that I do not include recipes. That's because there are many, many books and websites where you can find instructions for making whiskey cocktails as good as or better than anything I could offer. It's also because I wanted to explore the whiskeys themselves, and let you decide which ones sound like good candidates for a Manhattan. And besides, I love to sip well-aged rye neat, perhaps with a splash of water. "A rye thus kept becomes an evanescence, an essential grace," the historian Bernard DeVoto wrote. "It is not to be drunk but only tasted and to be tasted only when one is conscious of having lived purely."

How Whiskey Is Made

Reduced to its essence, whiskey is beer, distilled and aged in a wooden container. And like beer, it starts with grain. The percentages of different grains that go into a whiskey are called its mash bill; in the case of rye whiskey, rye makes up most of the mash bill. In Kentucky, most rye whiskey has a rye content between 51 and 55 percent; the rest is corn, with about 5 percent malted barley. MGP, the colossal distillery located in southern Indiana, across the Ohio River from Kentucky, makes most of its rye whiskey with a mash bill of 95 percent rye and 5 percent malted barley, though it has a few other standard mash bills as well. Pennsylvania rye typically uses a combination of unmalted and malted rye, or sometimes malted barley (wheat is common as well).

Before going further, what does "malted" mean, anyway, and why is there so much of it in whiskey? Grain is seed, of course, which, encouraged to pursue its biological wants, will sprout into a plant. As it does, it undergoes chemical changes, some of which occur before anything green emerges from the husk. Among those changes is the development of enzymes that help convert starch inside the seed into sugar, which is needed for fermentation.

Barley is the easiest grain to malt, so it is the most common, but rye distillers sometimes like to use malted rye instead. Corn is harder to malt, but malted corn is not unheard of. In any case, a little bit of malted grain goes a long way, which is why most bourbon and rye distillers use just 5 percent of it in their mash bill (though they might skip this step entirely in favor of artificial enzymes, an increasingly popular modern option). Unless they're looking for flavor, that's all they need.

Malted rye is a historically important component in American rye whiskey, in particular the Old Monongahela style. It steadily disappeared in the twentieth century, as the East Coast styles declined and rye production shifted to Kentucky, where distillers used malted barley instead.

Its return began on the West Coast, strangely enough. In 1993 Fritz Maytag, the owner of San Francisco's Anchor Steam Brewing, introduced Old Potrero, a pot-distilled, 100 percent malted rye whiskey—a throwback to the ryes of old. Since then a few more distillers have begun using it, from Coppersea in New York State to Dad's Hat, located outside Philadelphia, to New Riff, across the river from Cincinnati.

The malting process itself involves getting the seeds to start germinating, then quickly bringing the growth process to a halt before a plant emerges. The grain is steeped in water, then drained, then steeped again, a cycle that increases its moisture content without waterlogging it. A distiller might alternately spread the grain on a broad floor and spray it regularly with water while turning it frequently, a practice more common in Scotland than in the United States, though still found at tradition-oriented distilleries.

Once the grain has started to push out small rootlets, called "chits," it is time to dry it out, to arrest the germination process. This is done in a kiln, which is usually heated with natural gas. In Scotland the drying is sometimes done with peat, or semi-decomposed plant matter. When it burns, peat gives off a pungent, smoky scent, which gets into the grain and carries through distillation and aging. When you taste an Islay scotch, the peat is what makes it taste like iodine, seaweed, bandages, and so on. (Only a few distilleries in the United States use peat to make their whiskey, and none of the ryes in this book are peated.)

Regardless of the mash bill, the grains are milled and dumped into a large tank called a mash tub or cooker, where they get mixed with hot water. The resulting goopy mess is called the mash. At this stage, many distillers add a dollop of spent mash (called backset) from a previous batch, a technique called sour mashing. Doing so is energy-efficient, as the hot backset reduces the time needed to heat up the mash. More importantly, adding spent mash helps lower the pH level in the mixture, inhibiting the growth of unwanted bacteria. Almost all American whiskey is made with sour

mash, whether it includes those words on the label or not.
(The opposite of sour mash is sweet mash, a process used by
a handful of newer distilleries, notably Wilderness Trail and
Kentucky Peerless in Kentucky, who insist that it allows more
control over flavor development.)

In Scotland, after mashing, distillers separate the slick,
sugary liquid known as the wort from the solids before
fermentation. With a few exceptions, American distilleries
move it all, liquids and solids, from the mash tub to the
fermenter. There, along with the mash, distillers toss in
yeast, which eats the sugar and releases alcohol as waste.
Up until the early nineteenth century, most distillers relied
on whatever ambient yeast was in the air around them to
settle into the mash. Eventually, they learned to collect and
propagate certain yeast strains, the better to control for
consistency across batches and dial in certain flavors.

Though yeast doesn't come up in whiskey marketing
too often, it contributes an enormous amount to aroma
and flavor, and many distilleries keep their strains a closely
guarded secret, having developed them in-house and
maintained them for decades. Jim Beam, founder of the
eponymous distillery, is said to have collected his yeast in his
backyard in Bardstown, Kentucky, and was so protective of
it that he brought a small sample home every evening in his
car, so that if the distillery burned down, at least his precious
microorganisms would be safe.

These days many distilleries employ commercial yeasts,
which are easy to use but are bred more for efficiency than
flavor. A small but growing number of distilleries are going
back to using ambient yeast for their fermentation, though
they must be willing to accept variation in their batches,
ambient yeasts being multifarious and unpredictable.

Fermentation can take up to a few days, depending
on the yeast's voracity and the distiller's desires; a longer
fermentation produces more complex flavors. Fermenting
tanks are a sight to behold: Traditionally made from cypress
planks but today usually stainless steel, they are enormous,

often holding thousands of gallons. The liquid inside looks like a thin porridge, or something out of a witch's cauldron, bubbling away as the yeast gobbles up the sugar and starch and emits carbon dioxide along with alcohol. The level of alcohol can get as high as 10 percent, and eventually it kills off the yeast. Tragic, isn't it?

If you took that fermented mash, strained it, and tossed in some hops, you would have something very much like beer. In fact, many people call this stage distiller's beer, and some distilleries even use commercial beers as their base, rather than their own mash. To become whiskey, though, the alcohol content has to be significantly higher, which is where distillation comes in.

If you recall from chemistry class, distillation is the process of boiling a liquid compound, then separating the vapors based on the varied boiling points of the component liquids. In school, you probably would have used a few beakers and a Bunsen burner; in commercial distilling, you would use a still.

The still was invented by Arab scientists in the Middle East, and the device gradually found its way to Europe. The basic design is quite simple. A pot with a round, closed top is filled with fermented liquid and placed over a flame. Out of the top of the pot comes a metal tube, which coils up and then down into a receiving tank; the coils (or, in commercial distilling, a straight arm called a lyne), which sometimes pass through water, allow the vapor to condense. Stills are made mostly of copper, especially the tube—copper reacts with sulfur, a common and unwanted byproduct of whiskey distillation.

By paying attention to changes in the liquid coming off the still, a distiller can separate out water, alcohols, and other components, some of which are desirable, others poisonous. Typically, a distiller is focused on the "hearts," or the liquids coming off the still during the middle of the distillation run. Those at the first are called the "heads," and are usually collected, then redistilled. Those at the end are the "tails"; full of nastiness, they are usually discarded. Different distillers make their cuts differently, which results in different flavor profiles in their whiskey. Generally speaking, the broader the cut, the longer the whiskey needs to age, to allow all those trace elements at the beginning and end of the distillation to evolve and incorporate; the upside is that broader cuts, properly aged, produce more flavorful whiskey.

Stills made according to this basic design, known as pot stills, are popular in the United States and mandatory in Scotland for single malt scotch; there is a great romance to them, and they look beautiful. But they are not the only option, and in fact by volume, the vast majority of American whiskey (and American spirits generally) is made on what is called a column or continuous still. Several people invented versions of the column still in the early nineteenth century, but the one that ultimately took off was developed by a British customs agent named Aeneas Coffey.

The design is only slightly more complex than the pot still. Steam is pumped into the bottom of a hollow copper column, while a mash is pumped into the mid- or upper section. As the falling mash hits the steam, the vapors strip out volatile liquids (especially alcohol) and carry them toward the top, from which, as in a pot still, runs a condensing coil or lyne arm. A distiller controls the still by varying the level of heat and steam, as well as the flow of the steam, mash, and vapors through the use of corrugated metal trays inside the column.

There's one big, obvious advantage to the column still. It can be used continuously (hence one of its alternative names), whereas a pot still is run in batches, with messy, dangerous cleanup work in between. The downside to the column still is nuance—as in, it doesn't leave much behind. It is, in a way, too effective, which is why many new and small distilleries prefer the pot still, even with all its inefficiencies, or a hybrid still—essentially a column still on top of a pot still, which allows them to pivot between the two.

A third type of still, once common in rye distilling but

almost completely forgotten today, is the three-chamber still. It's something of a cross between a pot still and a column still. Instead of one continuous chamber, as in a column still, picture it divided into three chambers, stacked on top of each other. Mash sits in each of the chambers, having been pumped in from the top of the still. Steam is pumped in from the bottom, so that it bubbles through the mash in the lowest chamber. It then rises through a pipe at the top into the next chamber, and so on, until it leaves the still at the top. Eventually, the mash in the bottom chamber, now spent, is pumped out; the mash in the middle chamber passes to the bottom, to be replaced by mash from the top, which in turn is replenished by new mash.

The three-chamber still, sometimes made of wood, was the dominant equipment among rye distillers in Pennsylvania until the early or even mid-twentieth century, but it very quickly fell out of favor after Prohibition, and was just as quickly forgotten. In fact, when Todd Leopold of Leopold Bros., a distillery in Denver, approached Vendome, the renowned still manufacturer in Louisville, about making a three-chamber still, they went back and forth for years trying to recreate the design based on historical illustrations. It's easy to see why it fell from grace: Though it produces an unctuous, flavorful distillate, the three-chamber still is hard to control, and not nearly as efficient as a conventional column still. Then again, Leopold's three-chamber rye whiskey, which has won plaudits from critics, might bring the design back to its former glory.

Distillers usually run a liquid through a pot still twice: Once to strip out the bulk of what's unwanted, and again to fine tune the distillate. For column distillation, a distiller may run the liquid through one or two columns, and they often use a second, smaller, pot-like still called a doubler for the final refinement. What comes out at the end is often called whiskey, but it's not—it is distillate, or new make, or trybox, or white dog. To call it whiskey, it needs to age.

Distillers will debate whether 30 percent, or 60 percent,

or 90 percent of a whiskey's flavor comes from its time spent in a barrel, but all will agree that there is something fundamental to whiskey that requires prolonged contact with wood. Federal law requires that wood to be oak, and by tradition it is almost always white oak, though both law and tradition are predicated by practice: Oak is exceptional material for barrel-making, pliable but strong, full of whiskey-shaping compounds like tannins and vanillins, and white oak is especially abundant across the Eastern and Midwestern United States.

The standard barrel size is 53 gallons, but some craft distillers use smaller casks as well. The smaller the vessel, the higher the ratio of surface area to liquid volume, which means the faster the whiskey will take on barrel-imparted flavors and color. Few distillers will swear under oath to the superiority of small barrels; most use them to get whiskey to market faster while planning to move to full-size casks—which create more elegant, complex maturation flavors—as soon as money starts to come in. In truth, small barrels are like high-performance cars, effective but unforgiving. Even a few days too many in a small cask will make a whiskey taste like wood pulp.

Whatever the size, barrels must, again by law, be charred on the inside. A cooper sets a small fire inside a partially constructed barrel, usually for just a minute or so. Charring does not add flavor to the whiskey; rather, it adds color, as well as access, through its burnt ridges and furrows, to the wood deeper inside the cask. Typically, a barrel will have been toasted before it is charred, the better to coax and concentrate compounds in the wood, so that the alcohol and water in the whiskey can more easily reach them. At some point along most distillery tours, a guide will show off a used barrel stave, whose cross section will indicate just how deep whiskey can penetrate into the wood.

One of the many beauties of rye whiskey is that it blooms early. After just a few months in a barrel, young ryes are deliciously earthy, grassy, and herbal, with minimal barrel influence. Older ryes, as much as 20 years or more, are an entirely different spirit, with chocolate, mint, vanilla, and butterscotch. A good barrel manager knows how to identify barrels ready to dump early, and barrels to keep for the long haul, though until the advent of craft cocktails and craft whiskey, there was really not a market for very young ryes.

Regardless of how long a distillery wants to age its whiskey, it needs a place to put it. Smaller distilleries will often stick barrels wherever they can find space around their facility. Larger distilleries have separate warehouses, called rickhouses (or rackhouses). Hundreds of them dot the Kentucky countryside, marching up and down rolling hills like giant black cows.

Rickhouses vary in size and design. In America, they are typically multistoried, unheated, and built of an internal wood frame and an external cladding of wood, brick, or metal siding. Sometimes they are made of all brick; in a few cases, they're all metal, or concrete. Any decent whiskey maker understands that aging is as complex a process as distilling, if not more so, and uses the warehouse as an instrument to shape the evolving spirit.

One reason Kentucky has become a major whiskey-making region is its radical shifts in temperature, from winter to summer and even morning to afternoon, all of which drive the whiskey inside the barrels to slowly course in and out of the wood. In warm weather, the wood expands, sucking in the liquid; in cold weather the wood contracts, pushing the whiskey back out. As it does, the wood extracts unwanted compounds from the whiskey and imparts its own, enjoyable flavors. A barrel in Kentucky will lose about 5 percent of its liquid volume a year, colloquially called the angels' share. That's one reason why older whiskey is more expensive— there isn't much of it to sell.

As it ages and loses both alcohol and water through evaporation, the whiskey undergoes a series of chemical changes. The water and alcohol react with compounds in the wood, and all of them react with air in the barrel, creating new, more complex compounds that in turn greatly shape the aroma, flavor, and mouthfeel of the whiskey.

A good barrel-management team faces a constant challenge: to move or to leave. Different parts of a warehouse will have different microclimates—more or less humid, higher or lower temperatures. The warehouse, in this sense, is a tool, as important as a mash tub or still. Some distillers will keep their barrels in place; others, especially several large distilleries, will rotate their barrels to keep consistency. Leaving them in place has the advantage of creating different flavor profiles: Barrels filled with the same spirit on the same day will, if stored in different parts of a warehouse, produce very different whiskeys, because the slow press of different temperatures and humidity levels, over time, yields different results in the liquid.

There is a myth that until recently, distilleries often lost track of barrels. That may be true, especially in the pre-computer era when whiskey was unpopular and no one especially cared where the 7-year-old rye was resting. Those days are long gone, and now every barrel is accounted for, and then some, its dozens of data points tracked assiduously, so that distillers have no doubt when it is ready to dump.

Barrels are, of course, made of organic materials, as are their contents—so each barrel will age differently from the next, even if they hold whiskey made on the same day. For this reason, distilleries dump small or large batches of aged whiskey into vats, where they are allowed to mingle until they offer a consistent, coherent single flavor. In recent years, bars, retailers, clubs, and even individual fans have sought out "single barrel" whiskeys that have never been vatted together, paying a premium for access to a unique barrel, especially one that deviates ever so slightly from a familiar, prestige brand—Russell's Reserve (made at Wild Turkey), Knob Creek, and Wilderness Trail are all popular examples.

The aged and dumped whiskey is filtered and then typically brought down to a standard proof with water. Often distilleries use charcoal and chill filtration, the latter involving refrigeration to bring the whiskey low enough in temperature to solidify certain compounds which, though flavorless and harmless, can be unsightly if poured over an ice cube, as they give the liquid a cloudy tinge. Many distillers offer their whiskey without water added, so-called "cask strength" whiskey; others eschew even basic charcoal filtering to preserve the "fresh from the barrel" taste—which, these days, is in high demand.

Some distillers like to take the additional step of "finishing" their whiskey. After it has aged in new oak barrels, it is then re-casked in barrels that once held wine or other spirits, often port, sherry, or rum. Rye is, once again, especially fit for this step, its spicy, herbal character contrasting nicely with the sweet, decadent flavors of a typical finishing barrel.

History

Rye has come a long way. A grain that many people associate with dark bread and northern Europe originated as a domesticated crop in the Euphrates Valley, in present-day Syria and Iraq, about 10,000 years ago. It then slowly migrated north and west, across the Russian plains and into what would later become Poland, Germany, and the Baltic region. A hardy seed that grew well despite the harsh winters of its newfound home, its rough texture and bitter flavor made it for many a necessary but not especially beloved foodstuff. In his *Natural History*, Pliny the Elder, the Roman historian, philosopher, and military commander, calls it "a very inferior grain … only employed to avert possible famine." The people of northern Europe had a somewhat different opinion, and there it became a staple in everything from bread to beer to vodka and korn, a sort of "proto-whiskey" still made today.

Rye hopped across the Atlantic in the seventeenth and eighteenth centuries, in the hands of the first Dutch and German settlers. English settlers, who had mixed with Germans in London—then as now a cosmopolitan place—had likewise come to appreciate rye's versatility and vigor. As the historian David Wondrich has documented, among the earliest known instances of whiskey making in America came around 1648, when the English couple Emanuel and Lucy Downing established a small commercial distillery near Salem, Massachusetts., where they used both corn and rye in their mash. As Wondrich notes, it is often assumed that settlers like the Downings relied on Scottish and Irish distilling methods, but in a letter to a nephew back home just before opening his distillery, Emanuel asked specifically for the "German receipt for making strong water with rye meal."

Despite corn's reputed presence at the first Thanksgiving, it took until the end of the 1700s for it to emerge as a common staple crop in North America. In the often-rocky soils of the Atlantic colonies, it did not grow nearly as well as wheat, barley, and above all rye. Since rye seemed to grow wherever it was planted, it made a popular cover crop and an easy option for crop rotations. And as with any crop, farmers converted any excess rye on hand into whiskey, a high-value, easily portable commodity.

Although rum, made from molasses brought from the Caribbean as part of the transatlantic "triangle" slave trade, dominated colonial distilling, whiskey—which at the time meant any spirit made from grain—held its own as a popular drink during the Colonial era, especially among the inland and rural populations and the working class. Wealthier, urban colonialists drank madeira and other imported fortified wines; everyone else made and drank spirits from whatever they could afford or find, which in most cases was whatever local farmers had in surplus. Sometimes that was pears for brandy or apples for cider. But most often, it was grain.

Many of those early inland settlers were not English but Dutch, Swedish, and German, the last of whom arrived fleeing conflict in the Rhineland. They settled thickly in southeast and central Pennsylvania, up against the Appalachian Mountains and eventually over them, into the upper reaches of the Ohio River Valley. They coursed southward along the mountains' spine, blending with influxes of Scots-Irish settlers, planting the seeds, so to speak, of a grain-based distilling tradition that would eventually jump west into Tennessee and Kentucky.

The American Revolution brought an end to the triangle trade, and so an effective end to rum distilling in North America. It also brought a wave of patriotic egalitarianism, as wealthy, newly minted Americans found common cause with their brothers in arms by sharing their favored drink (conveniently, now the only drink they could find). Taverns, already hotbeds of Revolutionary activism, became political campaign grounds; John Adams wrote that, for better or worse, they had become "the nurseries of our legislators." After George Washington left the White House, he had a rye distillery built at his Virginia estate, run by a Scottish master distiller and at least two enslaved men as assistants. Working on five pot stills, they produced about thirty gallons a day. The distillery only ran for a few years, but during that time it was said to be among the largest sources of rye whiskey in the newborn country.

The Whiskey Rebellion

Washington's turn as a rye distiller was ironic given his treatment, while still in the White House, of his future fellow whiskey makers. The Revolutionary War had left the United States with massive debt, and under a scheme devised by Washington's secretary of the Treasury, Alexander Hamilton, the federal government assumed those debts incurred by the states in fighting the war. To pay them off, Hamilton created an excise tax on whiskey distilling, which Congress passed in 1791. Distillers could either pay the tax based on their annual capacity or on the actual gallons produced each year—a tough choice for rural distillers, who typically only ran their stills at harvest time, and who needed months to transport their product to market. That's if they sold it at all. Distilling is a great way both to concentrate the value of a grain harvest and to extend its life; grain can spoil, but whiskey can stay potable almost indefinitely. Add the fact that hard currency was scarce on the frontier, and it's no surprise that many western farmers used their whiskey as barter, trading for goods and services with a barrel or jug or two of rye whiskey.

Settlers heading west from Philadelphia would include a supply of whiskey among their stores—not to drink, but to trade once they crossed the mountains. "You would get your Conestoga wagon here, you would get your Kentucky long rifle here, and you would also get your whiskey," said Erik Wolfe, the co-founder of Stoll & Wolfe, a distillery in Lititz, Pennsylvania. "Once you went west or south, currency was pretty much useless, especially during the Revolution. If they had Maryland dollars or Massachusetts dollars, good luck spending it anywhere else."

To Hamilton and Washington, the distillers on the far side of the Appalachians may have seemed like isolated, ignorant hicks. But those farmers knew more about the world than many Eastern elites suspected. Among their demands for the new federal government in Philadelphia (Washington, D.C. had yet to become the capital) was the opening of the Ohio and Mississippi Rivers to trade. Given threats from Native Americans and the French and Spanish, who still controlled stretches of the rivers, they had a hard time moving their crops, and their whiskey, to ports like New Orleans and markets along the East Coast and in Europe. Not only did the new tax seem like a slap in the face from a federal government unwilling to protect their interests, but it seemed self-defeating and cruel: How were they supposed to pay the tax if they couldn't make enough money to do so in the first place?

Pittsburgh was, at the time, a small village around a military outpost, with just a few thousand people, depending on how you counted them, since it was not yet independent from the surrounding Allegheny County. But it was still the largest settlement in Pennsylvania west of the Appalachians, and it became the central point in what quickly turned into a popular uprising against the government's excise tax—and the first test of legitimacy for the newly founded republic. Resisters raised liberty poles, age-old symbols of independence that had sprouted around the colonies before and during the Revolution, and now refashioned as signs of opposition to the federal government. Farmers tarred and feathered tax collectors and chased off agents sent from Philadelphia with subpoenas.

A series of violent confrontations in and around Pittsburgh convinced Washington and Hamilton that a military response was necessary to put down what some partisans were styling a second American revolution, only this time with Washington as the far-off tyrant. Even today, Hamilton is a controversial figure in southwestern Pennsylvania, with his picture often hung upside down in disrespect. "You will see it in people's homes," said Ellen Hough, the co-founder of Liberty Pole Spirits, a distillery in Washington, about an hour south of Pittsburgh. "They say, 'Oh yeah, we had Alex upside down all our lives.' That's a Scots-Irish tradition. They turn the king and queen upside down to show a disrespect."

In August 1794, Washington declared western Pennsylvania to be in a state of insurrection, and sent in troops. With Hamilton in the lead, a federal army of almost 13,000 men arrived in western Pennsylvania that fall, and in November began arresting suspects, sometimes on little to no evidence. What has come to be known as the Whiskey Rebellion crumbled quickly. Twenty men were marched to Philadelphia for trial; twelve stood charged with treason. Two of them, John Mitchell and Philip Wigle, the namesake of Wigle Whiskey in Pittsburgh, were sentenced to death, though Washington, having made his point, later quietly pardoned them.

The Whiskey Rebellion stands as a great test of the new American republic, but its impact on the history of distilling is more complicated. Some writers claim that in the wake of the uprising, Pennsylvania farmers fled southwest along the Ohio River to resettle in Kentucky, seeding the new state with their knowledge of distilling. But as Michael Veach, the dean of American whiskey historians, has pointed out, while some families no doubt undertook that spiteful trek, they would have found thousands of farmers already making whiskey from the abundant crops of corn planted along the rich earth spreading north and south from the river.

Those who stayed left a greater legacy. Distilling had always been an everyday part of farm life, producing a commodity as interchangeable as cattle feed or bread flour. The rebellion, and the government's campaign to repress it, gave frontier distillers an identity. Suddenly, to make whiskey in western Pennsylvania was to participate in an activity imbued with political and cultural meaning, one that went beyond the particularities of mash bill and distilling technique.

The rebellion catalyzed the emergence of a regional sensibility around what would come to be known as Old Monongahela–style whiskey. Though records are sparse and inconclusive, Sam Komlenic, an expert on Pennsylvania's distilling history, says that Old Monongahela was defined by five characteristics:

> It was, first and foremost, made in and around the Monongahela River Valley. The river flows north from West Virginia to Pittsburgh, where it merges with the Allegheny to form the Ohio.
>
> It was a rye whiskey, made without corn and with a small amount of malted barley or malted rye.
>
> Distillers used a sweet mash, in which new yeast is added to ferment each batch—as opposed to sour mash, in which a portion of the spent mash from a previous batch is added to the next.
>
> It was made using a three-chamber still, a device in which pot stills are effectively stacked one atop the next to create something akin to the continuous distillation achieved in a true column still, while retaining the rich, round flavors produced by the pot still.
>
> It was aged in heat-cycled warehouses, which sped up the maturation process and gave the resulting whiskey a rounded, more vibrant flavor.

Long before Kentucky bourbon dominated the American whiskey scene, it was Old Monongahela that first gained national attention. In 1810, Pennsylvania produced 6.55 million gallons of whiskey, most of it rye; that same year Kentucky, making mostly corn-based whiskey, produced just 2.22 million gallons. And the "old" in "Old Monongahela" is important. At a time when most whiskey was consumed raw, the rye made in western Pennsylvania was typically aged, giving it a rich, red hue. "'Tis July's immortal Fourth; all fountains must run wine today!," Herman Melville wrote in 1851, in *Moby-Dick*. "Would now, it were old Orleans whiskey, or old Ohio, or unspeakable old Monongahela!"

The Overholt Saga

The story of Pennsylvania rye whiskey in the nineteenth century can largely be told through a single distillery and a single family. The Oberholtzers were German immigrants from the Rhineland region who had settled first near Philadelphia, then later migrated west toward Pittsburgh. Mennonites, they were not initially given to distilling—they mostly made rugs and other fabrics, in addition to farming.

But in 1803 Henry Oberholtzer, the reigning patriarch, set up a small still at the family homestead in the village of West Overton. Henry's sons Abraham and Christian expanded the distillery into a commercial operation, going from about seven gallons a day to about 200. Abraham later bought out his brother and inherited the farm, expanding whiskey production all the while.

He called his whiskey Old Farm Pure Rye, and its reach and reputation steadily grew, carried on flatboats down the Ohio—now firmly under U.S. control—toward New Orleans and east over wagon roads to New York and Philadelphia. According to Mark Meyer and Meredith Meyer Grelli, the authors of *The Whiskey Rebellion and the Rebirth of Rye*, it even reached California, where Gold Rush prospectors would ask for it in the saloons of the Sierra Nevada.

Business was so good that in 1859 Abraham, who had since anglicized his family name to Overholt, and his sons Jacob and Henry built a second distillery at a site along the Youghiogheny River, a place that George Washington, in his youthful days as a surveyor, had called Broad Ford. According to Komlenic, it eventually became one of the largest distilleries in the East, a colossal complex big enough to have its own company town across the river, reached by a footbridge. The Overholts later closed the West Overton distillery to concentrate their efforts at Broad Ford, but kept the original location for other purposes, including as a base for the region's nascent coke industry. Today it is a well-appointed museum, with a demonstration still that produces a small amount of its own whiskey.

The Overholts were not the only ones making whiskey in Pennsylvania: By the 1850s more than 1,000 distilleries were in operation, with a third of them in the area right around the Overholts' facilities. And while the Civil War temporarily shuttered distilleries in Kentucky, a border state, it proved to be a boon for Pennsylvania whiskey making, which supplied liquor to millions of Union soldiers and sailors.

Records are sparse and inconclusive, but historians believe that Pennsylvania rye was really two substyles. In the west, distillers relied solely on rye and wheat, while in the east, around Lancaster County, distillers used a good bit of corn, perhaps 25 percent (in both cases, malted rye or barley would have been used regardless). Such distinctions were more the result of necessity than any self-conscious desire to achieve distinction: Distillers simply used what was on hand. Corn was abundant in the east but scarce in the west. And in any case, Old Monongahela dominated the market, such that for many drinkers, it was synonymous with Pennsylvania whiskey regardless of its mash bill—at times synonymous with rye whiskey itself.

Abraham Overholt died in 1870, and ownership of the distillery passed to Henry Clay Frick, his grandson. Frick is best remembered as a steel and railroad tycoon—and as the benefactor of the Frick Collection, the august art museum in New York—but his first turn in business was as a young employee at Broad Ford. Later, after taking control, he brought on his friend and fellow tycoon Andrew Mellon as a partner. Together they continued to expand the distillery's operations, and in 1888 they renamed its flagship brand Old Overholt, after Frick's grandfather. Mellon especially loved the whiskey, and had crates of it delivered to his many homes. He only got through a fraction of his collection, so that even today bottles of pre-Prohibition Old Overholt appear regularly at auction, most of them drawn from Mellon's far-flung caches.

The turn of the last century was a boom time for American whiskey, among both its producers and its consumers. But it was also a wild time, especially before the Pure Food and Drug Act of 1906 brought some semblance of standards and transparency to the industry. Before that, anyone could call anything whiskey, and many a bartender or middleman added creosote and assorted oils to unaged, pure grain alcohol to make it look and taste like the real, more expensive thing. In response, distilleries like Old Overholt, which always made a high-quality aged product, looked for ways to distinguish their offerings as such. Whiskey advertising boomed, with companies touting the "pure," even "medicinal" qualities of their spirits. True or not, such marketing efforts helped lay the foundation for a modern whiskey industry built around well-recognized brands, Old Overholt among them.

Other innovations helped push the industry forward. Sealed bottles, filled by a distillery, gave customers assurance that they were buying actual whiskey; so did paper strips or seals placed over the closures. Automated bottling lines and bottle-making machines made it possible for distillers to dramatically boost their output, while the advent of mass-market newspapers and magazines got the word about their products to readers.

Most states along the Ohio River and in the mid-Atlantic made whiskey, but by 1910 Pennsylvania, Kentucky, and Maryland were the undisputed champs. All three produced a distinct style—Kentucky had bourbon, Pennsylvania had Old Monongahela, and Maryland had, well, Maryland rye. But whereas bourbon and Old Monongahela had relatively well-documented histories (after a point) with a clear sense of what went into them and a belief, true or not, that their authenticity relied on where they were made, Maryland rye was more nebulous. What made "Maryland Rye" was not its inputs, but its output: It tasted sweeter and smoother than Old Monongahela, a quality that might have been achieved through adding corn to the mash bill, but also, not infrequently, fruit juice or brandy to the spirit afterward.

Maryland rye was also insanely popular, especially in East Coast bars. H.L. Mencken, the Jazz Age scribe who loved Baltimore and booze in equal measure, spared no opportunity to praise his state's famous rye whiskey. It was, he said, "the most healthful appetizer yet discovered by man." The Mencken family doctor, he added, apparently approved: "He believed and taught that a shot of Maryland whiskey was the best preventive of pneumonia in the R months." In 1911 there were forty-four distilleries in Maryland, half of them in Baltimore, producing brands like Sherwood, Hunter, Mount Vernon, Monticello, and Braddock. Advertisements touted Maryland-style rye as a more refined alternative to its rougher cousins from Kentucky and Pennsylvania. And indeed it attracted a refined clientele: One ad, for a brand called Maryland Club, appeared in a leather-bound datebook recovered from the Titanic.

Decline and Fall

By the time of the Titanic's demise in 1912, however, Maryland rye was already starting to slip. Producers there and in Pennsylvania had been slowly losing out to the massive new distilleries erected along both sides of the lower Ohio River around the turn of the century, backed by investor money from Chicago and New York. Maryland distillers in particular, many of them located in crowded central Baltimore and therefore unable to expand, simply could not compete at a large enough scale.

The arrival of Prohibition in 1919 brought an end to many spirituous traditions in America, from the budding wine industry of California to the thousands of urban breweries spread across the Northeast and Midwest. When Prohibition was repealed, those local cultures and industries either failed to return or did so as pale corporate shadows of their former selves. Whiskey was a bit of both. The small distilleries that had made up the bulk of East Coast rye distilling never returned, their sites mothballed or converted to other uses, their employees drawn away to other lines of work. Kentucky, on the other hand, with its enormous distilleries and deep-pocketed interests, managed to hang on, however tenuously. Meanwhile a handful of companies—Schenley, Seagram, Hiram Walker, National Distillers—had gobbled up the lion's share of idled distilleries and aging barrels across the country. When Prohibition ended in 1933, those companies jumped back to life, but the rest of the American distilling industry, including much of Pennsylvania and Maryland, did not.

The problem was more than economic; this is not just a story of big money stomping out the smaller competition. It is also about trends in American gustatory culture. The twentieth century saw American consumers gravitate toward sweet and bland flavors and away from the rough, bitter, and spicy qualities common in nineteenth-century food and spirits. Bourbon—and blended scotch and Canadian whisky—were perfect fits for this newfound profile, with their sweet, smoother flavors. Rye, with its robust spice and herbaceous edge, had no place in that world. Eventually, so-called "white" drinks like vodka and white wine pushed out bourbon as well. Rye continued to have its adherents; as late as 1948, historian Bernard DeVoto could still assert, "I don't know why, but there are many more brands of good rye than there are of bourbon." But he was in a rapidly dwindling group.

Maryland distilleries, which investors bought for next to nothing during Prohibition, were soon being shut down and their parts and brand equity shipped west, the result of industry consolidation. A few held out. The last of them, Standard Distillers, did not close until 1983. Some brands, like Pikesville, continued to be marketed as "Maryland" ryes and sold mostly in the mid-Atlantic region, but they were made in Kentucky using corn-heavy rye mash bills. By the end of the millennium, Maryland rye had disappeared completely: Not only was it no longer made in Maryland, but its very existence was almost totally forgotten, and only a few old timers and hardcore aficionados could tell you what made it distinct.

The same story played out in Pennsylvania. A smaller and smaller number of distilleries made a smaller and smaller volume of whiskey for a smaller and smaller group of drinkers. Herman Mihalich, the founder of Mountain Laurel Spirits, a distillery outside Philadelphia, remembers his father carrying Old Monongahela at his bar in Monessen, south of Pittsburgh, but also recalls that by the time he reached adulthood, no one could tell him much about it. Erik Wolfe, the co-founder of the Stoll & Wolfe distillery, is a bit younger than Mihalich; by the time he was growing up in Lancaster County, he says, the region's rich distilling history was nowhere to be found. "Whiskey was born here, but growing up, you don't know that there was a whiskey tradition at all," he says.

The Overholts' distillery at Broad Ford was among the casualties. In the 1920s Mellon, who as secretary of the Treasury had to toe the line on Prohibition, had sold his controlling shares. They ended up in the hands of National Distillers, one of the new, all-devouring spirits companies that reshaped American distilling in the twentieth century through massive consolidation. National closed Broad Ford in 1951, never to be reopened or even repurposed; today it is a crumbling hulk, popular with graffiti artists and industrial archeologists but too far decayed to be salvaged. Unlike all but a few Pennsylvania whiskey brands (Rittenhouse is another), Old Overholt remained in production, though no one knows where. Even Komlenic, the leading expert in Pennsylvania rye history, is at a loss to say. What is clear is that, in 1987, National was acquired by Jim Beam, and production of Old Overholt shifted to Kentucky—and to the state's corn-heavy rye mash bill.

In 1989 Michter's, the last old-line distillery in Pennsylvania, and likely the last distillery of any noteworthy size on the East Coast, shut down. Its manager, Dick Stoll, had some forty years of experience in the industry, but without another distillery to hire him, he ended up working in road construction. It was the end of a 200-year tradition, and no one noticed.

Rebirth

And then, slowly, new shoots appeared. The Michter's brand was bought and relaunched as a Kentucky-based whiskey company with a deep portfolio of long-aged, delicious rye (and bourbon, too). In 2010 Mihalich, by training a chemical engineer and by trade a business executive, co-founded Mountain Laurel Spirits, the first distillery to make rye whiskey (under the name Dad's Hat) in Pennsylvania in twenty years. He was followed soon after by Wigle, in Pittsburgh, and within a decade by some 200 others. Wolfe even persuaded Stoll, long retired, to join him in a new distillery. The revival took a bit longer in Maryland, but today, Sagamore Spirit, Baltimore Spirits Co., and a dozen others are once more making rye whiskey in the state.

The rebirth of rye whiskey followed on the heels of the bourbon boom. Sales of American whiskey nearly doubled from 2011 to 2021, according to data from the Distilled Spirits Council of the United States, going from about 192 million bottles to about 360 million. There are any number of reasons bourbon took off: from the generational (Americans tend to latch onto whatever their grandparents found cool), to the alimentary (a renewed embrace of big, bold flavors after decades of bland), to the cultural (whiskey having played a starring role in 2000s hit shows like "Mad Men" and "Breaking Bad"). All of these are probably true, in some combination.

If bourbon's revival was driven by drinkers asking for it, rye's return began on the other side of the bar. Rye is one of the original cocktail spirits, much more so than bourbon, and as bartenders rediscovered classic recipes, they began reaching past bourbon and scotch for bottles of rye. What they found, at first, was dispiriting: Kentucky-style rye, with its heavy corn content, is very different from the rye once used to make Sazeracs and Rye Manhattans. Its sweet profile tends to get buried in a cocktail that relies on a robust, spicy rye to punch through other ingredients. And there wasn't much

of that rye, since established distilleries like Beam and Wild
Turkey distilled all the rye they needed for a year in a day
or two.

Fortunately for the nation's bartenders looking for big,
spicy ryes, there was not just one alternative source, but two.
Lawrenceburg Distillers Indiana (LDI), a massive distillery
across the Ohio River from Kentucky, made a 95 percent rye
mash bill (the remaining 5 percent is malted barley), and it
could churn it out at high volume. By the early 2010s, dozens
new ryes were starting to appear on the market, either as
brand extensions (Bulleit Rye, George Dickel Rye) or entirely
new names (Templeton); all of them were LDI whiskey,
bought and bottled by someone else. LDI was originally a
Seagram facility; it changed hands a few times before being
bought by a Kansas company called Midwest Grain Products,
which changed the distillery's name to MGP and later, in
2021, to Ross & Squibb. Even today, MGP produces a vast
amount of rye whiskey on the market, either through its own
brands or those of its customers.

The other early source for rye came from Canada. As the
story goes, Alberta Distillers in Calgary owned a vast portfolio
of very old, very delicious rye, which it had yet to blend into
traditional Canadian whisky and which it continued to sit on
even as the demand for rye whiskey began to take off in the
United States. A few enterprising Americans got wind of the
stash and started to buy it at bargain-basement prices, ship
it south, and bottle it as brands like Masterson's, WhistlePig,
and Lock, Stock & Barrel. Whether the Canadians were as
naïve as the lore would have them be is debatable; what
is not up for dispute is the whiskey itself—especially in its
first years, when farsighted buyers like Dave Pickerell, the
consultant who helped launch many of these early brands,
had their pick of the warehouse, and bottled some truly
outstanding whiskey that set the tone for what rye could do.

The same happened in Kentucky, where, starting in the
1980s, a small band of bottlers were putting out what many
consider the best American whiskey ever sold. Julian Van

Winkle, Even Kulsveen of the Willett Distillery, and Marci Palatella (best known for bottling a legendary brand called Olde Saint Nick), among others, were eking out a living by buying barrels of whiskey too old to blend into value brands like Evan Williams White Label, which at the time were the only things anyone would pay for. They had buyers overseas, and more importantly, they foresaw a day when American drinkers would return, not just to bourbon but to high-end bourbon, and to rye whiskey as well. Kulsveen in particular accumulated a near-mythic collection of barrels from Heaven Hill, Barton, and other distilleries—whiskey that he, and later his son Drew, put into bottles for brands like Michter's and Black Maple Hill. Van Winkle did the same for his customers, as well as for his own family brand, Old Rip Van Winkle. Some of these bottles today go for thousands, even tens of thousands of dollars. LeNell's Red Hook Rye, which the Kulsveens bottled for LeNell Camacho Santa Ana's liquor store in Brooklyn in the mid-2000s, now sells for north of $40,000 a bottle at auction. When it first appeared, it went for less than $100—and no one bought it.

The booming interest in, and continued allure of, rye whiskey soon persuaded craft distilleries to get involved too. It was easier said than done. As a mashed grain, rye is notoriously hard to work with. It tends to gum up easily, turning a mash that should have the consistency of thin oatmeal into something like a sticky blob of dough. But mastering rye was worth it to many distillers, who embraced not just the challenge but the opportunity to set themselves apart from the increasingly dense competition all making bourbon.

"When we started the distillery, more than 80 percent of the rye whiskey sold in Pennsylvania's state-owned liquor stores was produced by just two bulk distillers—MGP and Beam Suntory," Meredith Meyer Grelli of Wigle Whiskey said. "When everyone is buying bulk whiskey, you've got very little to play with to differentiate from a flavor perspective. You've knocked out differences in grains, in climate, in yeast, distillation, and fermentation methodology. All you have left is to determine how long to keep the whiskey in a barrel and what to proof it to. These, of course, have been the two primary marketing communications around whiskey since the industry consolidated with Prohibition."

Rye has another appeal to startup distilleries: Done correctly, it can be an absolutely stunning spirit with just a few years of age on it, full of herbal, grassy notes—unlike bourbon, which needs at least four or five years to cohere. That's great news for a new distillery pressed to get product to market. (Note I said "done correctly." There is lots of very bad young rye on the market, and getting it right with minimal time for the barrel to smooth over mistakes is no small task.)

The rye revival is readily apparent at West Overton, the seat of the Overholt family. Henry Clay Frick's daughter, Helen, preserved the homestead as a museum to her father; after she died in 1984, the site slowly shifted focus to its history as one of the fountainheads of American whiskey history. Today the complex, which includes the family residence, the distillery, and several worker dormitories, is a thriving museum. Across Pennsylvania, distilleries are not just making whiskey, and not just making rye whiskey, but resurrecting old styles and old methods, with an eye toward the day when Old Monongahela is once more called for by name at bars.

In a way, though, words like "resurgence" and "revival" do not completely capture what's going on. It's not a return to some earlier status quo, but a wholesale reimagining of what rye whiskey means and what can be done with it. In part that's out of necessity: There is much we don't know, and may never know, about rye-making a century or more in the past. Distillers have to make educated guesses about mash bills, fermenting times, distilling cuts, aging regimens. But from those guesses come innovations.

Distillers are embracing specific varietals of rye for flavor and suitability to their local climate: Leopold Bros. in Denver is partial to Abruzzi, a rye varietal that grows especially well in the South and the high mountain plains. Both Mammoth, in northern Michigan, and Stoll & Wolfe, in southeastern Pennsylvania, have embraced a varietal called Rosen, which was brought over from Europe around the turn of the last century, quickly adopted by rye distilleries across the country, and then just as quickly forgotten as rye slid from popularity. Rosen produces intense, rich flavors, but it cross-breeds easily with other varietals, so that farmers have to pay close attention to their crops—Mammoth is growing its initial harvests on a small island off the Michigan coast.

"From the 1920s to the 1960s the flavor of Rosen rye must have been ubiquitous not only in rye whiskey, but bourbon as well," said Ari Sussman, the master distiller at Mammoth. "In premium whiskey, grain inputs should be selected on the basis of flavor, not ease of handling or low cost. Rosen exemplifies this."

For a long time, distillers saw rye in a single dimension: spice. That's probably because in Kentucky, rye was and is mostly used as a flavoring grain, a supporting character that adds zest and depth to corn's friendly but superficial sweetness. Think of the way most people use black pepper to enhance other flavors, but rarely as a flavor in itself. That's starting to change as well.

A young rye whiskey abounds with herbaceous life, from vegetal earthiness to yeasty bread to sumac and funky tropical fruits; Willett's Family Estate 4-Year-Old and New Basin's Resignation Rye come to mind. Such whiskeys speak of a place, and a practice that reminds us that distilling is, at its core, an agricultural act.

Other distillers emphasize a different aspect of rye: its adaptability—specifically, how it makes an easy fit for barrel finishing. Unlike bourbon, which can often get lost in a wine-cask finish, rye takes those new notes in stride. To make a whiskey called Fortunato's Fate, New Liberty Distillery, in Philadelphia, finishes its 100 percent rye in sherry casks, harmonizing the whiskey's herbal, spicy character with the sherry's nutty and dried-fruit notes to produce something akin to fruit cake, but so much better.

"It came from a culinary inspiration," said Robert Cassell of New Liberty. "It doesn't work with bourbon, where you would have sweet on sweet. But if you have all this herbal spice that you can get from a rye and pair it with sweet, it's exactly what a chef would do in the kitchen."

If bourbon is one thing—variations on spicy sweetness— then rye is many things. A young rye tastes nothing like an older rye. Whiskey made from one varietal, in one place, will taste distinct from whiskey made somewhere else with a different type of rye. Some of rye's character and secrets have been known for centuries, and just need to be appreciated anew. Others have yet to be discovered. If America's new embrace of whiskey is not a fad but a return to form, a matter of the spirit finding its level, so to speak, then rye whiskey distillers still have a lot of time to show us everything the grain can do.

Rye's New Regions

The resurgence of rye over the last decade has meant a resurgence in regional styles as well. Pennsylvania rye distilleries are sprouting like weeds. Some, like Mountain Laurel and Stoll & Wolfe, are consciously historical in their approach, resurrecting the Old Monongahela style and sticking to it. Others, like Wigle, take rye as their base but innovate aggressively, making a wide range of barrel finishes and mash bills.

The rediscovery of Maryland rye as a style lags behind that of Pennsylvania, but the industry itself does not. The Old Line State is equally replete with startup distilleries, but they are working at a more fundamental level than their Pennsylvania neighbors—less interested in exhuming a specific historical style than in re-establishing a robust distilling industry in the first place.

New York has also seen a resurgence of rye distillation. In 2015 several distilleries in the Hudson Valley and elsewhere banded together to endorse Empire Rye, a new style of whiskey that, they claimed, harkened back to the way whiskey was made in the nineteenth century, when small distilleries dotted Upstate New York. They called the new style Empire Rye, and each of them agreed to release a product made according to its rules—among them that the whiskey has to use New York State–grown grain. It's an admirable effort, and the hope is that it will jump-start the evolution of a more specific rye style down the road. Similar branding efforts are underway in a handful of states, including Indiana, though again the specifics are broadly worded, the seed of a future style rather than a new style itself.

Such efforts might sound like marketing. If there's no real difference in production methods between New York and Indiana ryes, is there in fact any substantive difference to speak of? Right now the answer is no. But that could change. Think about these proto-styles as training wheels, programs that will get the state's distillers to start thinking of themselves as different, and to start finding ways to amplify those differences.

One thing that often goes unspoken when we talk about whiskey regions in the United States, at least for now, is terroir, a concept that is familiar in wine. Terroir simply means the influence that the land—including soil, climate, and water—has on a product. Vintners will drill down to the differences between acre-sized parcels in trying to explain why one wine tastes distinct from another. Not so with whiskey, and in part for good reason. Distillation is a harsh process that strips away many of the nuances of a grain, unlike fermentation, which is much gentler. And, at least in theory, the flavor of the grain is further diminished by the time spent in a barrel, where chemical interactions with wood and oxygen transform the whiskey's flavors into something entirely new.

At least, that's the traditional thinking. But a new generation of distillers is reconsidering that old orthodoxy, and nowhere more so than with rye whiskey. They make a couple of points. The first is that the lack of terroir in whiskey is a

Coppersea is one of the leading distillers behind the Empire Rye designation.

historical development, the result of using commodity grains, which have had their uniqueness bred out of them, and furthermore are sold all mixed together, so that whatever uniqueness a grain from one plot of land might have is wiped out by combining it with grain from thousands of other plots. But what if you went the other way, and distilled grain exclusively from one tract? High Wire Distilling, in Charleston, South Carolina, has sourced heritage grains for its bourbon and rye from different farms, and produced whiskeys with sizeable differences in nose and palate.

Wigle Whiskey is one of several new distilleries that insist on the influence of soil and climate on rye whiskey's flavor.

Second, proponents of terroir point out that the dominant grain in American whiskey, corn, is especially devoid of character. Not completely—there are some interesting whiskeys being made with heirloom corns. Corn, so the thinking goes, simply does not express where it's from.

Rye does. Wigle Whiskey ran an experiment where it bought the same varietal of rye grown in Saskatchewan, Minnesota, and Pennsylvania. It distilled and aged the batches separately, then ran chemical analyses on them. The differences were stark: The Pennsylvania rye, for example, had elevated levels of ethyl acetate, which imparts flavors like pear and bananas. They tasted different, too: The Saskatchewan whiskey is smooth and nutty, the Minnesota a bit earthy, the Pennsylvania fiery and fruity.

Far North Spirits, a farm-distillery located in Minnesota near the Canadian border, ran a similar experiment, but from a different direction. Working with the state department of agriculture, Mike Swanson, the co-owner and master distiller, planted adjacent plots of 15 varietals of rye, then distilled and aged each. He expected to find differences, but he was still surprised by the magnitude of variety among the resulting whiskeys, especially after they spent time in a barrel.

"Rye has some flexibility to it," Swanson told me. The challenge now, he said, is for distillers to figure out how to work with that flexibility. "What does it mean that a rye is from a certain part of the country? Can we can we start characterizing regional expressions of rye, or even distillery-specific expressions?"

It's something farmers and distillers once understood but have since forgotten. But like fifteenth-century engineers rediscovering the building secrets of the Romans, they are learning it all over again. If that's not the definition of a renaissance, what is?

Mike Swanson of Far North Spirits ran an experiment growing and distilling different rye varietals on his Minnesota farm. The results astounded him.

How to Drink Whiskey

I'm often asked how to drink whiskey. What I want to say is: the same way you would drink anything else. But of course, there's a subtext to the question. What people mean to ask is, what is the right way to drink whiskey? What is the ritual? What will impress the bartender, and what will draw stink-eye stares?

There is both one correct way, and no single correct way, to drink whiskey—in both cases, it's however you want. It's your drink, you paid for it (or someone bought it for you), and the entire point of imbibing is to enjoy it. If you need an ice cube or a splash of water or cola to do so, by all means do it. Snobs may scoff, but if you're drinking to impress them, you're playing a losing game.

With that said, if you are drinking not just to enjoy but to evaluate a whiskey, I do have some pointers—techniques I use when I am on a judging panel or I just want to assess a whiskey.

Before we get to the actual assessment, let's talk equipment: glassware, specifically. If you're just drinking to enjoy, anything goes. But to get a good sense of the whiskey, you're going to need a glass that amplifies the aromas, otherwise called the nose. There are some types of glasses designed specifically for nosing and tasting whiskey, the Glencairn glass being the most widely used. It is relatively thin, with a wide base and a narrow neck and mouth, and a solid base. But really, any similarly proportioned glass will work about as well: a red wine glass, a brandy snifter. I swear by a set of stemless cabernet glasses.

You should never store your whiskey in a refrigerator, but in any case you want it at room temperature before you drink it. Cold will encourage certain compounds in the whiskey to solidify, altering the flavor. Needless to say, you don't want to add an ice cube to a whiskey you're about to analyze, and if you add water later (we'll get to that), the water should be room temperature as well. To that end, it helps to have an eyedropper to add precise amounts of water, but it's not strictly necessary.

The only other thing you might want to have on hand is a notebook or sheet of paper, to take notes. You'll want separate line entries for smell (nose), taste (palate), swallow (finish), and general comments. You might add entries for mouthfeel and color as well.

When you're ready to smell, don't shove your nose in the glass. Treat a whiskey you don't know like a dog you don't know. Sure, it's friendly, but if you stick your face in its face, you're likely to come back with a little less face. Alcohol is volatile, meaning that it vaporizes easily. Plus, everyone's olfactory sensitivity is different; some people need to stick their nose right up to a whiskey to smell it, while others can pick up odors from several inches away.

Regardless of how precise a sense of smell you have, I recommend starting from a good distance away, then slowly bringing the glass toward you until you can smell enough without the vapors stinging your nostrils. Don't rush through this stage; take some time to pick out details and nuances.

The Glencairn glass is ideal for tasting whiskey, with its solid base, wide bulb (to let the whiskey breathe) and thin mouth (to concentrate aromas).

If at first you smell spices, think: What kind of spices? If it's cinnamon, what kind? Free associate: If it smells like Red Hots, say so. (You'll probably want to write all this down.)

When it comes to tasting, first impressions don't count. You should take a quick sip to acclimate your mouth to the whiskey; even a relatively mild whiskey is at least 40 percent alcohol. Then, on the second sip, try to think in three stages. First, what does it taste like right when it hits your lips? The whiskey is still cool and the flavors compact. What are those initial impulses? Start broadly. Ask yourself: Is it sweet or spicy? Is it floral? Is it robust, or reticent?

Once you have the whiskey all in your mouth, let it sit there. Swirl it around a bit, so it hits all your taste buds. With your lips closed, open your mouth, to give the whiskey room to expand. I mean this literally: As it warms to your body temperature, the alcohol will start to evaporate, changing the flavor of the whiskey, what some people call the "turn." How do those changes register to you? Does it grow spicier? More robust? Or does it flatten out?

Finally, swallow, and concentrate on how the whiskey tastes as it hits the back of your mouth and goes down your throat. Is it smooth, or does it burn? And is there much of an aftertaste? Does it linger, or shut off?

If you need to, try it again. As you do, go back to those initial notes and expand on them. If the entry was spicy, what kind of spice? Sweet, like cinnamon candy, or peppery, like a chile? Again, don't be afraid to free associate—that's the fun of it all.

None of this is strictly necessary to enjoy whiskey. Many people will find it fussy, and that's okay. I recommend it simply as a way to structure your thoughts about the drinking experience, and to move from saying simply "I like it" or "I hate it" to explaining why you like or hate it—and using that assessment to seek out similar whiskeys, and to avoid others. The chart on pages 48–49 offers a sample of typical tasting aromas and flavors of rye whiskey.

Drinking Together

There's nothing wrong with a quiet drink by yourself, but there's nothing more fun than drinking with friends. Here are a few tips for organizing a whiskey tasting.

The whiskey: If you're providing the drinks, try to have a variety on hand. If it's going to be a rye night, have a Kentucky style, a Pennsylvania style, an MGP, a barrel proof, and a finished rye, for example. Or go for a theme: all ryes from Maryland, or only finished ryes.

The accompaniments: You'll want some water, both for drinking and for adding to the whiskey itself. An eye dropper is good to have on hand. You'll want napkins and a dump bucket or cup, for those who wish to taste but not heavily imbibe. And get some snacks, both as palate cleansers and as stomach-fillers. Stay away from anything too flavorful, especially anything too spicy or salty. Roasted nuts, mild cheeses, dried fruits, and unsalted crackers are always good choices.

Notes: Optional, but if you're going to get nerdy, make sure everyone has a pencil and paper to write down their impressions. If you want to go all out, make score sheets ahead of time with prompts for nose, palate, finish, general notes, and a score.

Don't go crazy: All that said, a tasting should be fun. The more formal and complicated you make it, the more it will feel like work, and the less people are going to enjoy the whiskey or your company.

Typical Tasting Aromas and Flavors

WINEY	WOODY	SULPHURY	FEINTY
Sherried	**New wood**	**Vegetal**	**Sweaty**
Chardonnay	Sandalwood	Brackish	Yeast
Port	Ginger	Cabbage water	
Applejack	Black pepper	Stagnant	**Tobacco**
	Allspice	Marsh gas	Dried tea
Nutty	Nutmeg		Pipe tobacco
Almond	New oak	**Coal-Gas**	Tobacco ash
Marzipan	Chile pepper	Cordite	
Salted nuts	Mint	Ash	**Leathery**
Chesnuts	Cumin	Matches	Leather
Pumpkin seeds	Hickory		upholstery
Toasted almond	Cinnamon bark	**Rubbery**	New cowhide
Caraway seeds	Cedar wood	Pencil eraser	Saddle leather
	Cumin	Oak dust	
Chocolate	Clove		**Honey**
Cream	Buttery oak		Clover honey
Butter	Spicy oak		Beeswax
Milk chocolate	Clove		
Cocoa	Spearmint		
Bitter chocolate			
Chocolate	**Vanilla**		
mousse	Caramel		
Dark chocolate	Toffee		
Fudge	Brown sugar		
	Molasses		
	Maple syrup		
	Nougat		
	Butterscotch		
	Custard		
	Toasted		
	Coffee		
	Coffee grounds		
	Fennel		
	Fennel		
	Aniseed		

SMOKY	FLORAL	FRUITY	CEREAL
Wood fire	**Perfume**	**Citric**	**Mash**
Hickory smoke	Marigold	Orange	Porridge
Char	Honeysuckle	Tangerine	Cheerios
Mesquite	Rose	Orange zest	
	Lavender	Lemon zest	**Cooked**
Medicinal		Meyer lemon	**Vegetable**
Iodine	**Greenhouse**	Orange peel	Sweet corn
Band-Aid	Geranium		Corn chips
	Cut flowers	**Fresh Fruit**	Plump corn
		Apple	
	Hay	Pear	**Husky**
	Mown hay	Peach	Dried hops
	Dry hay	Apricot	Ale
	Dried herbs	Banana	Pancakes
	Herbaceous	Strawberry	
	Wheatgrass	Raspberry	**Meaty**
		Cherry	Boiled pork
			Pork sausage
		Cooked Fruit	Grilled pork
		Stewed apple	
		Marmalade	
		Jam	
		Barley sugar	
		Candied fruit	
		Glacé cherries	
		Dried Fruit	
		Raisin	
		Fig	
		Dried apricot	
		Prune	
		Fruit cake	
		Solvent	
		Bubblegum	
		Wood varnish	

How to Read a Rye Bottle

Interpreting a whiskey label can be deceptively hard. Some bottles will display a lengthy declaration and backstory about the contents, others are terse or cryptic, while others plainly state the case. On the opposite page is an example of a whiskey label with a good deal of information. Below are annotations by me regarding elements on the label.

NAMES The label states that it is a "Straight Rye Whiskey." To be considered "straight," it has to be made in a single state and aged at least two years. If it is between two and four years old, the precise age in months has to be stated. To be considered a "rye whiskey," it has to contain at least 51 percent rye in its mash bill, and it has to be aged in new, charred oak barrels.

AGE STATEMENT This label states that the whiskey is 10 years old, which technically means that it is at least 10 years old—there may be older components in it, but the youngest component is 10 years old. Not all whiskey carries an age statement, which does not, in all cases, reflect the quality of the drink. Older whiskey tends to be more expensive for obvious reasons—it was stored for a long time and a good deal of it will have evaporated each year.

PLACE OF DISTILLATION On the front or back, a bottle must provide the state or states where the whiskey was distilled. Unless this is a point of pride for the brand, it will usually be provided in very small print.

ALCOHOL BY VOLUME / PROOF By law, all whiskey bottles must state the level of alcohol by volume. Often this is abbreviated as Alc/Vol. This whiskey is botted at 46.4 percent alcohol by volume. Some bottles also include proof, which in the U.S. is simply double the alcohol by volume. Whiskey is available from a minimum of 40 percent Alc/Vol (80 proof) and up. Proof can be a measure of value for money, since most whiskey leaves the barrel at a very high proof and is diluted with water before bottling.

LIQUID MEASURE By law, liquor bottles for sale in the U.S. must somewhere display the measurement of their contents in metric values. (In the case of this bottle, it is printed on the side.) Whiskey is most popularly sold in bottles labeled 750ml (milliliters), which converts to a little over 25 U.S. ounces. This measurement equals one-fifth of a gallon and thus, a "fifth" of whiskey. Of course, both larger and smaller bottles of whiskey are also available on the market.

Whiskey
Accounts

About the Accounts

The "Whiskey Accounts" section of this book is organized by maker and/or brand in alphabetical order. Included for each is background and historical information about the company that offers the whiskey to consumers. For brands that distill their whiskey, the account gives their city and state. For brands that source their whiskey, the account lists "no location." This is because most distilling producers have visitors centers and/or some sort of connection to their location—think Jim Beam's home in Clermont, Kentucky—while the vast majority of non-distilling producers do not.

Each "expression" (that is, individual offering) has its own tasting notes, separated into text regarding mash bill, if available, nose, mouthfeel, and palate (including finish), as well as general notes about the whiskey.

In the upper right corner of the entry is the amount of alcohol by volume (ABV) in the whiskey and, when known, its age. At the bottom center is the price with dollar signs corresponding to the following range of costs:

$ = $30 or less
$$ = $31–$50
$$$ = $51–$100
$$$$ = $101 or more

I have based the dollar amounts from average prices found in both my local shops and as advertised on the internet for the bottles pictured in the accounts.

The vast majority of whiskeys covered in this book are sold in a standard 750ml measure and the prices indicated are for this size of bottle. You may find bottles that cost much more or less than the range of prices I have indicated. These are strictly estimates. And like so many things in life, price is not always commensurate with value.

Rating whiskey is a vastly subjective undertaking. I have included ratings as an indication of my own personal taste, informed by the members of our tasting panel. A low mark for a whiskey does not make it "bad." I just don't like it, and don't recommend it.

My ratings are also driven by my own desire to figure out which whiskeys I value more than others, which to avoid, and why. There are so many whiskeys to try and hopefully, so much time to figure it all out. With this in mind, the ratings in this book follow this scale:

★★★★ = Phenomenal
★★★ = Excellent
★★ = Good
★ = Decent; some flaws, but drinkable
NR = Not recommended

While not every whiskey in this book will be available in every store or state, I have attempted to build as near-comprehensive a list of the regular-production, "core range" expressions available from distilleries on the market. Some expressions have been discontinued, but I've kept them in the book because bottles are still plentiful, and I believe they're worth seeking out.

45th Parallel Distillery

NEW RICHMOND, WISCONSIN

"49th Parallel" is a 1941 movie starring Lawrence Olivier, written to drum up American support for the allies in World War II. 45th Parallel is a distillery located in tiny New Richmond, Wisconsin, east of Minneapolis. Like the movie, 45th Parallel is slow—though in this case, it's a virtue. "We don't do anything fast," its website proclaims, which includes a long fermentation and a commitment to extended maturation. The distillery gets its grain from a local farm, and sells its spent mash to a nearby cattle ranch, which will eventually produce fertilizer for future crops, creating a nice, slow circle of life.

45th Parallel New Richmond Straight Rye

65 percent rye, with the rest of the mash bill split between corn and barley

AGE	**4** years old
ALC/VOL	**46**%

NOSE	MOUTHFEEL	FINISH
Caramel, oregano, nectarine, shortbread, orange juice	Light to medium	Medium; fruity

GENERAL	PALATE
There are some fun things about this whiskey, but it's a bit too soft in the palate.	Soy sauce, raisins, black pepper, mushrooms, with a very dry finish

PRICE	RATING
$$$	

Angel's Envy

LOUISVILLE, KENTUCKY

Angel's Envy was founded by Wes Henderson and his father, Lincoln, a legendary distiller for the spirits company Brown-Forman. Lincoln had recently retired, and Wes suggested they go into business together. Lincoln had dabbled in cask finishes and wanted to do more—and the rest is history. Angel's Envy debuted in 2013 with a bourbon finished in ruby port casks, to rave reviews. Lincoln Henderson passed away the same year, but he got to see their dream come to fruition as one of the most successful new whiskey companies in Kentucky. Wes sold the company to Bacardi in 2015 and stepped down in 2022, passing on management to his son Kyle.

Angel's Envy Rye

95 percent rye and 5 percent malted barley; finished 18 months in rum casks

AGE	No age statement
ALC/VOL	**50**%

NOSE	MOUTHFEEL	FINISH
Pipe tobacco, green curry, mace, Szechuan pepper, molasses, almond paste	Medium to full	Long; cinnamon

GENERAL	PALATE
Complex and full-bodied. The port influence is obvious, with a big hit of holiday spices thrown in.	Fruit cake, nutmeg, dark chocolate, toffee, cherry, and port

PRICE	RATING
$$$	★★

Balcones Distilling

WACO, TEXAS

Balcones is one of the oldest distilleries in Texas, having gotten its start in the late 2000s, when Texas whiskey still sounded like an oxymoron. But then, Balcones has always been a little different, right down to the Portuguese-made still that its founder, Chip Tate, insisted on installing. Later, under the direction of master distiller Jared Himstedt, the Waco-based distillery grew rapidly, thanks to its popular line of single malt whiskeys and bourbon made with Texas blue corn. It released its first rye whiskey, made on a pot still, in 2018.

Balcones Rye

100 percent rye mash bill, blending Elbon rye with crystal, chocolate, and roasted rye malts

AGE		
No age statement		
ALC/VOL		
50%		

NOSE	MOUTHFEEL	FINISH
Vegetal funk, mango, coffee grounds	Light to medium	Mango, coffee

GENERAL	PALATE	
There are some interesting things going on here, but the aggressive tropical funk will be a turnoff for most.	Cocoa powder, coffee beans, tropical fruits	
	PRICE	**RATING**
	$$	

Baltimore Spirits Co.

BALTIMORE, MARYLAND

Founded by three friends in 2015, the Baltimore Spirits Co. is dedicated to reviving the city's nearly forgotten legacy as a hotbed for whiskey making and drinking. Before Prohibition, dozens of distilleries dotted Baltimore and its environs, many of them making Maryland-style rye whiskey. Baltimore Spirits makes more than just whiskey, though—its portfolio includes gin, amaro, and several types of apple brandy.

Epoch Straight Rye

BATCH 7

70 percent rye and 30 percent malted rye

AGE

3

years old

ALC/VOL

63.2%

NOSE	MOUNTHFEEL	FINISH
Feed sacks, leather, dill, linseed oil	Medium	Medium; chocolate

GENERAL	PALATE
A rough-edged and rowdy rye, like a horse that isn't fully broken yet. It's pleasantly unique, but not for everyone.	Cinnamon, chocolate, mint, cooked grain

PRICE	RATING
$$	

Barber Lee Spirits

PETALUMA, CALIFORNIA

Barber Lee is one of several relatively new distilleries to emerge as an adjunct to an established winery. In this case, Lorraine and Michael Barber, the wife-husband team behind Barber Cellars of Sonoma County, California, decided to branch out into making rye whiskey, but soon realized there aren't enough hours in the day to do both. Fortunately, they found a partner in Aaron Lee, a fan of the winery who quickly agreed to join as their distiller. Like the winery, Barber Lee uses locally sourced ingredients and basic, low-tech production methods to emphasize the agricultural origin of the whiskey.

Barber Lee BATCH 2
Single Malt Rye

100 percent malted rye; a blend of 1½, 2, and 3-year-old whiskeys

AGE
No age statement

ALC/VOL
45%

NOSE
Cheese, acetone, popsicle stick, ginger ale

MOUTHFEEL
Medium

FINISH
Minty and sweet

GENERAL
Grain-forward and youthful, like it wants to be a single malt more than it wants to be a rye, but ends up missing both targets.

PALATE
Butterscotch, peppermint, wet grains

PRICE
$$

RATING
NR

Belfour Spirits

NO LOCATION

Ed Belfour made his name as one of the best goaltenders in the history of the National Hockey League, primarily with the Chicago Blackhawks and the Dallas Stars. Looking for something to do after retirement, he founded an eponymous whiskey brand with his children Dayne and Reaghan. Unlike some celebrity brands, Belfour and his family are hands on, learning the trade and doing much of the work themselves. So far, they have made whiskey at distilleries in North Carolina and Colorado, bottling it in Louisville.

BelfourRye

70 percent rye, 20 percent corn, and 10 percent malted barley

AGE	ALC/VOL
2 years old	**47**%

NOSE	MOUTHFEEL	FINISH
Resin, instant oats, clove, dried grain	Light	Medium; oregano and Juicy Fruit

GENERAL	PALATE
Zesty and vivacious, a good example of a solid, youthful rye whiskey.	Pine, licorice, eucalyptus, roses

PRICE	RATING
$$$	

Black Button Distilling

ROCHESTER, NEW YORK

Jason Barrett grew up working in his grandfather's button factory in Rochester, but it wasn't a career option—Barrett is color blind, making it a challenge to produce anything besides black buttons. So he turned to whiskey, opening his distillery in 2012, one of the first in western New York. Black Button is best known for its bourbon, but its Empire Rye has been a brisk seller.

Black Button Empire Straight Rye

95 percent rye and 5 percent malted barley

AGE		No age statement
ALC/VOL		**42**%

NOSE	MOUTHFEEL	FINISH
Beeswax, linseed oil, green banana	Light	Medium; tannins

GENERAL	PALATE	
The flavors are consistent, balanced, and full. It's young, but that youth is all about herbs and spice rather than washed-out grain.	Butterscotch, peppermint, wet grains	
	PRICE $$$	**RATING** ★★★

Black Dirt Distillery

WARWICK, NEW YORK

Black Dirt was founded in 2012 at the Warwick Valley Winery, located just north of the New York–New Jersey border. It takes its name from the region's fertile, dark soil, which has supported farming for thousands of years. The whiskey took off, and in 2013 co-founders Jason Grizzanti and Jeremy Kidde built a separate, 4,000-square foot distillery nearby, where they produce both whiskey and applejack. The distillery was purchased by Proximo Spirits in 2018.

Black Dirt Straight Rye

90 percent rye and 10 percent malted rye

AGE	**3** years old
ALC/VOL	**50**%W

NOSE	MOUTHFEEL	FINISH
Lemon-lime soda, banana, leather	Full	Short; confectioners' sugar

GENERAL	PALATE
Well integrated and straightforward; it lacks complexity but makes good use of what it has.	Pine, licorice, eucalyptus, roses

PRICE	RATING
$$	★★

Black Maple Hill Whiskey

NO LOCATION

Black Maple Hill debuted in 2000, reportedly using whiskey sourced from Stitzel-Weller and bottled by Julian Van Winkle III for a California-based importer called CVI Brands. A few years later, Kentucky Bourbon Distillers (aka Willett) took over bottling, and reportedly sourced the whiskey from Heaven Hill. Both versions were delicious, and highly sought-after. But when finding old Kentucky bourbon and rye grew challenging, CVI switched sources to a craft distillery in Oregon called Stein. In everything but name, it's an entirely different product: Even the bottle is different, going from tall and slender to short and squat.

Black Maple Hill Straight Rye

75 percent rye and 25 percent corn

AGE No age statement		
ALC/VOL **47.5**%		

NOSE	MOUTHFEEL	FINISH
Feed store, raw peanuts, hay, dill, celery seed	Medium to full	Long; cinnamon

GENERAL	PALATE
A well-made, grain-forward rye. It's young but competent and balanced.	Batter, grain, Juicy Fruit, celery, red licorice

PRICE	RATING
$$$	

Blaum Bros. Distilling Co.

GALENA, ILLINOIS

The pride of Galena, Blaum Bros. was founded in 2013 by Mike and Matt Blaum. They're best known for a limited, annual release called Oldfangled Knotter bourbon, a blend of whiskeys sourced from MGP, usually around seven years old. But they make their own juice, ranging from vodka and gin to rye and a much younger bourbon.

Blaum Bros. Straight Rye

92 percent rye, 5 percent smoked malted barley, and 3 percent malted barley

AGE		
4 years old		
ALC/VOL		
50%		

NOSE	MOUTHFEEL	FINISH
Dill, anise, maple-glazed ham, chicken soup	Medium	Long; lingering heat

GENERAL	PALATE
A traditional, straightforward rye; simple—in a good way.	Cinnamon, chocolate, ginger, barbecued meat

PRICE	RATING
$$	★★ ◀

Blue Run Spirits

NO LOCATION

One of several NDP brands to debut during the Covid-19 pandemic, Blue Run stands out from the pack with its distinctive, butterfly-bedecked packaging and, more importantly, its close affiliation with distilling legend Jim Rutledge. While getting his own distillery up and running, Rutledge has consulted for several brands; for Blue Run he selected barrels for its first few releases and oversaw production on its new-make whiskey, which is contract-distilled. Blue Run bottles at cask strength, and while characteristics vary from batch to batch, they tend toward big, rich, and sweet profiles.

Blue Run Golden Straight Rye   FALL 2021 BATCH

Undisclosed mash bill

AGE
No age statement

ALC/VOL
47.5%

NOSE	MOUTHFEEL	FINISH
Lemon, oregano, dill, celery salt, meatloaf, wet leaves	Light-medium	Medium; black tea

GENERAL	PALATE
A perfect holiday whiskey; good on a cold day, like drinking a fruit cake.	Fruit cake, cinnamon, plum, strawberry jam, walnuts

PRICE	RATING
$$$$	

Bone Snapper Rye

NO LOCATION

Bill Kennedy and Nolan Smith founded Bone Snapper in 2011 as a sourced whiskey brand, bottled at high proof. Originally available in just Indiana and a few other states, it can now be found around the country. In addition to its regular-release rye, Bone Snapper also offers X-Ray, a 4-year-old rye so named because, at that age, it is said to offer a deeper look into the "bones" of the whiskey.

Bone Snapper Rye

95 percent rye and 5 percent malted barley

AGE **4** years old		
ALC/VOL **54**%		

NOSE	MOUTHFEEL	FINISH
Faint, tobacco, char, Lemon Pledge	Medium to full	Medium; butter-scotch

GENERAL	PALATE	
The nose is shy and it loses points for that, but the whiskey itself is delicious, with so much to give—it tastes well-aged and well-rounded.	Butterscotch, apple candy, horehound, molasses	
	PRICE $$	**RATING** ★★

Boondocks Craft Whiskey

NO LOCATION

Dave Scheurich is among the most experienced and lauded distillers in America, having worked at Seagram, Wild Turkey, and Woodford Reserve, which he helped create in the mid-1990s. After retiring, he hung out a shingle as a consultant. He teamed up with the Royal Wine Co. to create Boondocks, an NDP brand for which he selects and blends well-aged whiskies for its bourbon and rye.

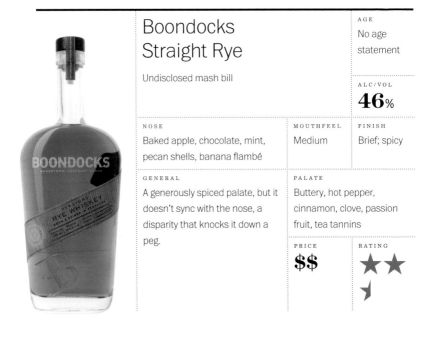

Boondocks Straight Rye

Undisclosed mash bill

AGE		
No age statement		
ALC/VOL		
46%		

NOSE	MOUTHFEEL	FINISH
Baked apple, chocolate, mint, pecan shells, banana flambé	Medium	Brief; spicy

GENERAL	PALATE	
A generously spiced palate, but it doesn't sync with the nose, a disparity that knocks it down a peg.	Buttery, hot pepper, cinnamon, clove, passion fruit, tea tannins	
	PRICE	RATING
	$$	★★

Boone and Crockett Club Whiskey

NO LOCATION

Long before he became a Rough Rider, president, and Nobel Peace Prize laureate, Theodore Roosevelt was a conservationist. In 1887 he co-founded the Boone and Crockett Club, a group of big-game hunters and outdoorsmen dedicated to preserving America's natural heritage—as much a concern in the late nineteenth century as it is today. The club licenses its name to a line of whiskies, including a bourbon, blended whiskey, and rye.

Boone and Crockett Club Straight Rye

Undisclosed mash bill

AGE No age statement		**ALC/VOL** **43**%
NOSE Tropical fruit, vanilla, coconut meat, Demerara syrup	**MOUTHFEEL** Light	**FINISH** Medium; astringent
GENERAL Intriguing, unique nose, but the palate is too tight and thin.	**PALATE** Butterscotch, apple candy, horehound, molasses	
	PRICE **$$**	**RATING** ★★

Boone County Distilling

INDEPENDENCE, KENTUCKY

Boone County, in northern Kentucky, was a hotspot for whiskey distilling in the late nineteenth century, and home to the Petersburg Distillery, which at one point produced 4 million gallons of whiskey a year—more than all but the largest of today's distilleries. Prohibition cut off distillation in Boone County, and it didn't restart until 2015, when Boone County Distilling opened near the historic Petersburg site. Among other distinctions, Boone County is one of the only distilleries in the country to have its entire operation certified kosher by the Orthodox Union.

Boone County Small Batch Straight Rye

95 percent rye and 5 percent malted barley

AGE No age statement		
ALC/VOL **45.4**%		

NOSE	MOUTHFEEL	FINISH
Port, dried figs, chicken broth, toasted marshmallow, blueberry jam	Medium	Short; pepper-mint

GENERAL	PALATE	
Full of rich herbal amaro flavors, this drinks like a Black Manhattan. Well matured and intricately balanced.	Mint chocolate, ginger, dill, raisins, Luxardo cherry	
	PRICE $$	**RATING**

Bower Hill Whiskey

NO LOCATION

The Battle of Bower Hill was the only violent engagement of
the Whiskey Rebellion, and its name is memorialized in this
sourced whiskey produced in Louisville. Bower Hill whiskey
is widely available and reasonably priced, but very little is
known about its ownership or production.

Bower Hill Reserve Straight Rye

Undisclosed mash bill

AGE		
No age statement		
ALC/VOL		
43%		

NOSE	MOUTHFEEL	FINISH
Clove, caramel, char, fennel, dill, spiced cider, cigar box	Thin	Short; astringent

GENERAL	PALATE
Nose is warm and spiced, roasted, and toasted, but the palate is a bit of a comedown—tight and superficial.	Orange peel, peach cobbler, honey, almond oil

PRICE	RATING
$$$	

Braddock Oak Whiskey

PURCELLVILLE, VIRGINIA

Made by the Catoctin Creek distillery in Virginia, Braddock Oak is available exclusively at Total Wine & More, a major liquor store chain. Unlike some private-label brands that are sourced from large distilleries and bear anonymous profiles, Braddock's roots at Catoctin Creek make it worth seeking out.

Braddock Oak Single Barrel Rye

100 percent rye

AGE	ALC/VOL
No age statement	**46%**

NOSE	MOUTHFEEL	FINISH
Horehound, licorice, dark cherries, pine, tarragon	Light	Short; spiced oak

GENERAL	PALATE
Young, crafty, and fragile—just a few drops ruin it. But what's there is alluring and promising of things to come with a little age.	Coffee, toasted grain, linseed, oatmeal, cedar, peanut saltiness

PRICE	RATING
$$	★★⭒

Breuckelen Distilling

BROOKLYN, NEW YORK

When the Great Recession brought carnage to the New York finance world, Brad Estabrooke, a rookie bond trader, decided it was time to change careers. He turned to whiskey, and in 2010 he founded Breuckelen Distilling, using the original Dutch spelling for Brooklyn, where he set up shop. Estabrooke does everything a little different: His bourbon is made with wheat, not rye, while his single malt is aged in new oak barrels.

Breuckelen 77 Bonded Rye

100 percent rye

AGE	**4** years old
ALC/VOL	**50**%

NOSE	MOUTHFEEL	FINISH
Perfume, talcum, dill, lemon, sweet tobacco	Light	Long; anisette

GENERAL	PALATE
Clean and sweet, especially for an American rye—it drinks more like a Canadian whiskey.	Caraway, dill, mint, sweet citrus

PRICE	RATING
$$$	

Breuckelen 77 Local Corn and Rye

90 percent rye and 10 percent corn

AGE	**4** years old
ALC/VOL	**50**%

NOSE	MOUTHFEEL	FINISH
Tangerine, potpourri, amaretto, red bean paste	Light to medium	Light to medium

GENERAL	PALATE
A compelling nose and entry, but it fades too quickly. It leaves you wanting a resolution, like a play without a final act.	Caraway, dill, mint, sweet citrus

PRICE	RATING
$$$	

Buffalo Trace

FRANKFORT, KENTUCKY

Among the most iconic alcohol brands in America, Buffalo Trace is also one of the most historic—even though the name is relatively new. Distilling has taken place on its site near downtown Frankfort since the late eighteenth century, and since then it has occupied the careers of some of the state's best known whiskey men, including Col. E.H. Taylor, Jr., George T. Stagg, Albert Blanton, and Elmer T. Lee. Like many of the state's largest distilleries, Buffalo Trace is best known for its bourbons, but it produces a fair number of rye whiskey expressions as well, some of which, like Van Winkle Family Reserve Rye (page 177) and the Antique Collection (including Thomas H. Handy and the 18-Year-Old Sazerac), are almost impossible to find thanks to limited production and skyrocketing consumer demand.

Thomas H. Handy Straight Rye 2018 RELEASE

Undisclosed mash bill, but it contains rye, corn, and malted barley

AGE
No age statement

ALC/VOL
64.4%
Varies

NOSE	MOUTHFEEL	FINISH
Pineapple, orange peel, pickled watermelon, green tomatoes	Full	Long; spicy

GENERAL	PALATE
Thick, rich, and chewy, this is a noble beast of a rye—complex, evolving, and balanced from start to finish.	Dark chocolate, roasted nuts, dried chiles, root beer, hops

PRICE
$$$$

RATING

Sazerac Straight Rye

Undisclosed mash bill, but it contains rye, corn, and malted barley

AGE		
6 years old		
ALC/VOL		
45%		

NOSE	MOUTHFEEL	FINISH
Honey, cherry tobacco, antique store, oranges	Medium	Medium length; fruity, herbal, and grainy

GENERAL	PALATE
Easy drinking and pleasant; young and fruity; a good all-around pour.	Chewy and oak-forward; grainy, with mint and menthol

PRICE	RATING
$$	★★★

Sazerac 18 Year Old Straight Rye   2018 RELEASE

Undisclosed mash bill, but it contains rye, corn, and malted barley

AGE		
18 years old		
ALC/VOL		
45%		

NOSE	MOUTHFEEL	FINISH
Walnut, cherries, vermouth, leather, dark chocolate	Medium	Short; astringent

GENERAL	PALATE
Starts off strong but it's downhill from the nose. The palate could be better balanced, and the finish is so wispy as to be barely there.	Polished oak, chocolate-covered cherries, coffee beans, dried blueberries

PRICE	RATING
$$$	★★★

Buffalo Trace Kosher Straight Rye

Undisclosed mash bill, but it contains rye, corn, and malted barley

AGE	
7 years old	

ALC/VOL	
47% years old	

NOSE	MOUTHFEEL	FINISH
Guava tang, spearmint, toasted grain, acetone, tobacco leaves	Light-medium	Short; leather

GENERAL	PALATE
Inoffensive and enjoyable; an unchallenging rye that rises above the median in its competence.	Orange peel, cedar, honey, ginger ale, lemon

PRICE	RATING
$$$	

Bulleit Frontier Whiskey

SHELBYVILLE, KENTUCKY

Tom Bulleit created his eponymous brand in 1987, claiming that he used the same mash bill that his great-great-grandfather had employed in the mid-nineteenth century. He had it made on contract at what is now Buffalo Trace, and later sold it to Seagram. The brand ended up in the hands of Diageo, the British spirits giant, which continued sourcing the whiskey until it opened the massive Bulleit Distillery in Shelbyville, east of Louisville. (A second, even larger distillery was added later in Lebanon, to the south, though Bulleit rye has been and continues to be distilled by MGP.) Though Bulleit is marketed as "frontier whiskey," it is designed for urban drinkers, with a balanced palate that works neat and in cocktails.

Bulleit 12-Year-Old Straight Rye

95 percent rye and 5 percent malted barley

AGE	
12 years old	
ALC/VOL	
46%	

NOSE	MOUTHFEEL	FINISH
Honey, almonds, mint	Light-medium	Mint, cola and, at the end, floral; lingering

GENERAL	PALATE
Bracingly conventional rye, but a bit thin. It doesn't take water well.	Butterscotch, Big Red gum, vanilla

PRICE	RATING
$$	★★

Bulleit Straight Rye

95 percent rye and 5 percent malted barley

AGE	
No age statement	
ALC/VOL	
45%	

NOSE	MOUTHFEEL	FINISH
Coffee, vanilla, lemon pepper, leather	Medium	Medium, with molasses, mint, and bitters

GENERAL	PALATE
Young and unbalanced, but with unique notes and layers of complexity.	Tangerine, chocolate-covered cherries, astringent, orange zest

PRICE	RATING
$	★★

Buzzard's Roost Whiskey

LOUISVILLE, KENTUCKY

Jason Blauner, the owner of Bourbon's Bistro, knew that his Louisville restaurant had to have a strong whiskey program to thrive in the Derby City. Since opening its doors in 2005, Blauner has run a prolific barrel-pick program, which allowed him to forge bonds with some of the state's top distilleries, large and small. A decade later, he used those skills and relationships to create Buzzard's Roost, a sourced brand of bourbon and rye.

Buzzard's Roost Single Barrel Straight Rye

95 percent rye and 5 percent malted barley

AGE	ALC/VOL
No age statement	**52.5**%

NOSE	MOUTHFEEL	FINISH
Sweet tobacco, black tea, orange slice, banana	Light	Long; treacle

GENERAL	PALATE	
Sharp, perhaps too much so, with some off notes on the nose. Still, there's a lot to like, especially over a rock.	Honey, coconut, milk chocolate, roasted nuts, Lipton's iced tea	

PRICE	RATING
$$$	

Castle & Key Distillery

FRANKFORT, KENTUCKY

The site where Castle & Key now sits was once one of the most resplendent of Kentucky distilleries, Old Taylor. After E.H. Taylor departed what is now Buffalo Trace in the 1880s, he pulled out all the stops to build his next distillery. Modeled after a Rhenish castle, it featured the latest in distilling technology, as well as a sunken garden and manicured lawns. Prohibition ended Taylor's dream, and for decades the distillery sat unused. But new investors came along in 2014, and today the distillery, with all-new equipment as well as a new name, is making whiskey under contract for a variety of brands, including Pinhook, as well as its own releases.

Castle & Key Restoration Rye   BATCH 1

63 percent rye, 20 percent malted barley, and 17 percent yellow corn

AGE	No age statement
ALC/VOL	**51.5**%

NOSE	MOUTHFEEL	FINISH
Oatmeal, vanilla, rubber, hint of smoke, maple candy	Medium	Quick; fruit

GENERAL	PALATE
There are signs of good flavor initially, but the intense woodiness and overall weird chemical notes crowd them out.	Aspirin, Lemon Pledge, fruit cocktail, tongue depressor

PRICE	RATING
$$	 ★★

Catoctin Creek Distilling Co.

PURCELLVILLE, VIRGINIA

Nestled in the foothills of the Shenandoah Mountains northwest of Washington, D.C., Catoctin Creek has been making whiskey since 2009. Becky and Scott Harris, the wife-and-husband team behind Catoctin, came to distilling from industrial chemistry (Becky) and programming (Scott)—very different skill sets that nevertheless suited them well for making spirits, which even at the craft level is a complex, exacting operation. Along with their regular-run rye, in 2021 they released Ragnarök, a very limited-edition whiskey made in collaboration with the metal band GWAR. Catoctin Creek is also the source distillery for the Braddock Oak brand, a private label of Total Wine & More stores.

Catoctin Creek Roundstone Cask Proof Rye

100 percent rye

AGE		No age statement
ALC/VOL		**58%**

NOSE	MOUTHFEEL	FINISH
Orange oil, marzipan, sweet smoke	Full	Barrel char, cinnamon stick

GENERAL	PALATE	
This is a big, complex whiskey, heavy on the spice and so much fun to piece apart.	Orange, Atomic Fireball, roasted almonds, dry	

PRICE	RATING
$$$	

Cedar Ridge Distillery

SWISHER, IOWA

Iowa is not usually thought of as a distilling state, but as the country's largest producer of corn, it should be. At least that's according to the Quint family, who founded the Cedar Ridge winery in 2005 and started making whiskey in 2010, becoming the state's first licensed distillery since Prohibition. Cedar Ridge uses locally sourced grains, including heritage corn, to produce its single malt, bourbon, and rye whiskies. It also makes a blend of straight bourbon and straight rye called No. 9 Reserve in collaboration with the metal band Slipknot, another Iowa native.

Cedar Ridge Straight Rye

51 percent malted rye, 34 percent rye, 12 percent corn, and 3 percent malted barley

AGE	**4** years old
ALC/VOL	**43**%

NOSE	**MOUTHFEEL**	**FINISH**
Dried grass, pineapple, Naugahyde, eucalyptus, brown sugar	Light	Short; bitter

GENERAL	**PALATE**
A restrained, wispy whiskey that as a whole seems more like a Canadian rye than an American.	Dill, rye bread, marigold, grass, pine, beeswax, gooseberry.

PRICE	**RATING**
$$	

Charleston Distilling Co.

CHARLESTON, SOUTH CAROLINA

Originally located in Charleston's historic downtown district, the Charleston Distilling Co. relocated in 2019 to John's Island, a western suburb, where it occupies a $4.2 million, 10,000-square foot facility. The former location could produce about 50 barrels' worth of whiskey a year; the new space, with a 45-foot column still, can make that much in two weeks. Like many new distilleries, Charleston prides itself on buying local, using only grains grown in South Carolina for its whiskies, gin, and vodka.

Charleston Distilling Crosstown Straight Rye

100 percent rye

AGE
No age statement

ALC/VOL
50%

NOSE	MOUTHFEEL	FINISH
Caramel, bubble gum, root beer, mint toothpaste	Light	Medium; herbal

GENERAL	PALATE	
A well-done but unremarkable young rye. It has a delicately floral palate, but it lacks a defined spine and a clear finish.	Cinnamon, fennel, lavender, chocolate Necco wafers	

PRICE	RATING
$$	

Chattanooga Whiskey

CHATTANOOGA, TENNESSEE

The city of Chattanooga, about halfway between Atlanta and Nashville, used to have 30 active distilleries. But when Chattanooga Whiskey opened in 2011, it was the first legal distillery in the city in a century. The company is best known for its Tennessee High Malt, an incipient bourbon sub-style that uses a heavy dose of malted barley.

Chattanooga Straight Rye Malt

Mash bill percentages undisclosed, but it uses pale malted rye, caramel malted rye, chocolate malted rye, and yellow corn

AGE	
3 years old	

ALC/VOL
49.5%

NOSE	MOUTHFEEL	FINISH
Peach candy, brown sugar, coffee candy, lemon pepper	Medium	Medium; black tea

GENERAL	PALATE
Lots to love here. It's a master-class in dark rye notes, and they evolve the longer it sits in the glass.	Tobacco, lemon pepper, coffee, dill, mint, clove

PRICE	RATING
$$	

Chicken Cock Whiskey

PARIS, KENTUCKY

Chicken Cock traces its roots to 1856. The brand was among the most popular whiskies made during the industry's late nineteenth-century golden age. It sold especially well in the West, but also in East Coast nightclubs, most notably the Cotton Club in Harlem. But Chicken Cock was one of many whiskeys to be mortally wounded by Prohibition, the distillery shuttered and the brand archived. Fast forward to 2011, when Matti Anttila, the founder of Grain & Barrel Spirits, brought it back. Chicken Cock is now distilled at Bardstown Bourbon Co.

Chicken Cock Straight Rye

95 percent rye and 5 percent malted barley

AGE	No age statement
ALC/VOL	**45**%

NOSE	MOUTHFEEL	FINISH
Vanilla, perfume, roses, cantaloupe, dried honeycomb	Full	Medium; metallic

GENERAL	PALATE
It's lovely but fragile; even a few drops of water will ruin it. But as it is, it sings.	Cola, wood char, grilled herbs, honeysuckle, lime, elderflower

PRICE	RATING
$$$	

Cleveland Whiskey

CLEVELAND, OHIO

Whiskey makers have always been on the hunt for a way to speed up the aging process, and Cleveland claims to have found it. The company places 6-month-old whiskey and several wood staves in a pressure tank, and it claims that over a few days it can use that pressure to replicate the movement of whiskey in and out of the wood, a process that usually takes years.

Cleveland Underground Rye Finished with Black Cherry Wood

95 percent rye and 5 percent malted barley

AGE	No age statement
ALC/VOL	**45**%

NOSE	MOUTHFEEL	FINISH
Papaya, Necco wafers, burlap, linen, lemon icing	Medium	Short; tannic

GENERAL	PALATE
Serviceable—the nose is shy, but the palate is alluringly complex, and makes for a great cocktail component.	Lemon peel, clove, cinnamon, ginger, tangerine

PRICE	RATING
$$	★★

Clyde May's Whiskey

TROY, ALABAMA

The family of Clyde May claims that he was the most wanted moonshiner in postwar Alabama. His signature twist was, according to his descendants, to add apple cider to his whiskey, a step the family replicated when it relaunched the whiskey in 2001. The brand sources its whiskey, but is working to build a distillery in Troy, Alabama, the first distillery of any significant size in the state.

Clyde May's 8 Year Old Straight Rye

Undisclosed mash bill

AGE	**8** years old
ALC/VOL	**47**%

NOSE	MOUTHFEEL	FINISH
Sweet pipe tobacco, butter-scotch, apricots, old paneled wood room	Full	Medium; spicy chocolate

GENERAL	PALATE
A chewy, layered, conventional rye, mature and balanced. It's on the dry side, but still full of flavor.	Brown sugar, dried ginger, saltwater taffy, dark chocolate, cinnamon

PRICE	RATING
$$	

Clyde May's Straight Rye

Undisclosed mash bill

AGE		
No age statement		
ALC/VOL		
45%		

NOSE	MOUTHFEEL	FINISH
Coal ash, malt, pumpernickel, peanut skins, chalk	Full	Brief; cocoa

GENERAL	PALATE
Dry, chewy, dessert-like, but also explosively robust. It's a bit strange, but compelling.	Floral, cocoa, talcum, vanilla, honey

PRICE	RATING
$$	★★

Cooperstown Distillery

COOPERSTOWN, NEW YORK

Located on the shore of Otsego Lake in central New York, Cooperstown is located in the same town as the Baseball Hall of Fame. Not surprisingly, much of its iconography is baseball-related—its bourbon is named for Abner Doubleday, the reputed (if disputed) founder of the sport, and it sells baseball-shaped decanters and bottles. Despite the hype, it is a true craft distillery, drawing most of its grain from nearby farms.

Cooperstown Select Straight Rye

Undisclosed mash bill

AGE		
No age statement		
ALC/VOL		
41%		

NOSE	MOUTHFEEL	FINISH
White Shoulders perfume, white chocolate, earthy, coconut husks	Full	Brief; cocoa

GENERAL	PALATE
Dry, chewy, dessert-like, but also explosively robust. It's a bit strange, but compelling.	Floral, cocoa, talcum, vanilla, honey

PRICE	RATING
$$	★★★

Copper Fox Distillery

SPERRYVILLE, VIRGINIA

Rick Wasmund caught the distilling bug on a trip to Scotland. An internship at the Bowmore Distillery followed, and in 2005, he founded Copper Fox, one of Virginia's first craft distilleries. Though many others have since opened, the distillery remains one of the most tradition-bound in the state—most of its grain come from a single, nearby farm; its whiskeys are distilled on a copper pot still; and it is one of the few distilleries in the country to floor-malt its own barley. It is also unique in using a heavy bit of applewood to smoke its barley and age its whiskey.

Copper Fox Original Rye

66 percent rye and 34 percent malted barley; matured in ex-bourbon barrels with toasted applewood and oak chips, making this not a true rye.

AGE		
No age statement		
ALC/VOL		
45%		

NOSE	MOUTHFEEL	FINISH
Leather, cedar, fenugreek, burnt rubber, grain silo	Medium	Short; coffee

GENERAL	PALATE
Pungent and phenolic, like a wet campfire. It's intriguing, but a bit overwhelming.	Wood, coffee bean, gamey, smoky, cinnamon candy

PRICE	RATING
$$	

Copper Pony Rye

NO LOCATION

Copper Pony, like Winchester Rye (see page 246) is a house brand sold at Total Wine, a major big-box wine and liquor retailer. The whiskey is produced by the Green River Spirits Co. (formerly Terressentia), a company headquartered in South Carolina that claims to speed up the aging process using a proprietary method it calls TerrePURE.

Copper Pony Rye

Undisclosed mash bill

AGE	No age statement
ALC/VOL	**45**%

NOSE	MOUTHFEEL	FINISH
Dill, musk, lemon, burlap sack	Light	Long; spice

GENERAL	PALATE
It's sweeter than the nose implies. Light and gentle, it errs too far on the delicate side and ends up tasting thin and flat.	Celery, maple, cherry cough syrup, grilled tropical fruit

PRICE	RATING
$$	★

Coppersea Distilling

NEW PALTZ, NEW YORK

Coppersea Distilling sits on the outskirts of New Paltz, just south of the Catskill Mountains. Its founder and head distiller, Christopher Williams, embraces many of the traditional methods common among the multitudes of distilleries that once called the Hudson Valley home. He floor-malts locally sourced grain, ferments in open-top tanks with ambient yeast, and distills the liquid using a direct-fired copper still. The unaged spirit enters the barrel at a low 105 proof, resulting in a rich and fruity whiskey. Coppersea was a founding member of the Empire Rye consortium.

Coppersea Bonticou Crag Straight Rye Malt

100 percent malted rye

AGE	ALC/VOL
No age statement	**48**%

NOSE	MOUTHFEEL	FINISH
Hoppy, violets, Leo candy sticks, potpourri, fresh cut pine, cinnamon stick	Light to medium	Short; citrus

GENERAL	PALATE
A young rye, with the wood and spice profile of a craft whiskey. It actually works better with a few drops of water, which seem to tie its varied notes together.	Fruit cake, rye, cereal, Mexican chocolate, coffee, a touch of smoke

PRICE	RATING
$$$	

Coppersea Excelsior Straight Rye

80 percent rye and 20 percent malted rye

AGE

No age statement

ALC/VOL

48%

NOSE

Fresh dill, nutmeg, graphite, linseed, oiled canvas

MOUTHFEEL

Medium

FINISH

Brief; coffee grounds

GENERAL

A Pandora's box of aromas and palate notes. Not bad individually, but they don't always gel, like a band with good players who can't sync.

PALATE

Hay, Play-Doh, bergamot, tea, port, spiced wine

PRICE

$$

RATING

Corbin Cash Distillery

ATWATER, CALIFORNIA

People rarely associate California's lush Central Valley with distilling—this is food crop country. In fact the Souza family, which owns the Corbin Cash distillery, has been growing sweet potatoes and other vegetables near Merced for over a century. When John David Souza took over the family farm, though, he recognized that turning some of those crops into alcohol was a great way to diversify the business, and have fun doing it. Not surprisingly, many of Corbin Cash's spirits incorporate sweet potatoes, including a vodka and a liqueur, as well as its blended whiskey, which combines the sweet potato distillate with its 100-percent rye whiskey.

Corbin Cash Merced Rye

100 percent rye

AGE	ALC/VOL
No age statement	**45**%

NOSE	MOUTHFEEL	FINISH
Horehound, blond tobacco, menthol, dill	Light to medium	Long; citrus peel

GENERAL	PALATE		
Complicated and soft, it's missing depth and richness—all treble, no bass.	Floral, dry apple cider, ash, cigar, rosemary, fennel		
	PRICE	RATING	
	$$		

Corsair Distillery

NASHVILLE, TENNESSEE

Founded in Bowling Green, Kentucky, in 2008 by two childhood friends, Darek Bell and Andrew Webber, Corsair was one of the South's first craft distilleries. When the company moved to Nashville two years later, it became the city's first distillery since Prohibition. Corsair occupied one end of an old auto factory on the edge of downtown, sitting alongside an antique shop and another distillery, Nelson's Greenbrier. Early on, Corsair was known for its prolific innovation, with sometimes a dozen or more spirits in production. But eventually Bell and Webber settled on a core line, including two types of gin, a single malt, and a rye.

Corsair Dark Rye Malt

61 percent malted rye, 4 percent malted chocolate rye, and 35 percent malted barley

AGE	ALC/VOL
No age statement	**42.5**%

NOSE	MOUTHFEEL	FINISH
Orange zest, Cognac, cinnamon-banana pancakes, ginger ale	Light	Medium; sweetly spicy

GENERAL	PALATE
A pleasant pour that would benefit from a higher proof; as-is, it is too frail to support its range of flavors.	Oatmeal, sweet cinnamon, orange Creamsicle, Andes mint

PRICE	RATING
$$	★★⯪

Crater Lake Spirits

BEND, OREGON

In operation since 1996, Crater Lake is one of the oldest craft distilleries in the country, a fact even more notable given its location in rural Bend, Oregon, on the eastern side of the Cascade Mountains. The distillery was originally best known for its gin and vodka, but as of late it has pushed into whiskey. Among its offerings has been Black Butte American malt whiskey, made in collaboration with the Deschutes Brewery, located just down the street.

Crater Lake Rye

100 percent rye

AGE No age statement		
ALC/VOL **40**%		
NOSE Roasted walnuts, toasted wheat, licorice, mint	**MOUTHFEEL** Thin	**FINISH** Medium; bitter
GENERAL Too young and raw; it needs more time in the barrel to work out what it wants to be.	**PALATE** A good bit of heat, with wet cereal, carboard, and mint	
	PRICE $	**RATING**

Dad's Hat Rye

BRISTOL, PENNSYLVANIA

Dad's Hat, made at Mountain Laurel Spirits in the northern Philadelphia suburbs, is leading the push to reinvigorate Pennsylvania's rye whiskey scene. Co-founder Herman Mihalich did years of historical research into the production and characteristics of what was one of the most distinctive spirits made in America, but which had almost completely disappeared by the postwar era. Mihalich grew up watching his father and grandfather drink rye, and sing its praises, so after a career in business, in 2006 he pivoted to distilling. Rye is all that Dad's Hat makes, though in a variety of expressions and finishes.

Dad's Hat Straight Rye

80 percent rye, 15 percent malted barley, and 5 percent malted rye

AGE	**4** years old	
ALC/VOL	**47.5**%	

NOSE	MOUTHFEEL	FINISH
Dill, caramel, turpentine, herbal, dried cedar, green apple	Light	Short and minty

GENERAL	PALATE
Tight and tannic; an uptight whiskey.	Lots of dill, mint, burnt orange, vegetal, baking chocolate

PRICE	RATING
$$	★★

Dad's Hat Rye Finished in Vermouth Barrels

80 percent rye, 15 percent malted barley, and 5 percent malted rye

AGE
No age statement

ALC/VOL
47%

NOSE
Mint, pine, caramel, dill

MOUTHFEEL
Medium

FINISH
Lingering white pepper and mint

GENERAL
A likeable sipper, with a pine and mint freshness that carries through the nose and palate.

PALATE
Mint, cola, raspberry, licorice

PRICE
$$

RATING
★★★

Dad's Hat Bottled-in-Bond Rye

80 percent rye, 15 percent malted barley, and 5 percent malted rye

AGE
5
years old

ALC/VOL
50%

NOSE
Bell pepper, menthol, grassy, and bushels of dill

MOUTHFEEL
Medium

FINISH
Oaky and drying; soft and pleasant

GENERAL
A great expression of fresh, herbal qualities of a young rye. It's singular, and alluring.

PALATE
Palate: Spicy and chewy, with dill, spearmint, black pepper, brown sugar, and Mexican chocolate

PRICE
$$$

RATING
★★★

Dad's Hat Straight Rye

80 percent rye, 15 percent malted barley, and 5 percent malted rye

AGE		
No age statement		
ALC/VOL		
45%		

NOSE	MOUTHFEEL	FINISH
Dill, caramel, dried wood, apple blossom, mint, musky	Light	Lingering; cherry cough drops

GENERAL	PALATE	
Tight and unbalanced; aggressively bitter, but with some classic rye character.	Dill, medicinal mint, burnt orange, cedar, pine sap	
	PRICE	**RATING**
	$$	

Dad's Hat Rye Finished in Port Wine Barrels

80 percent rye, 15 percent malted barley, and 5 percent malted rye

AGE	
No age statement	
ALC/VOL	
57%	

NOSE	MOUTHFEEL	FINISH
Mothballs, leather, dill, caraway seed, coffee beans, barrel char	Medium	Medium; pepper

GENERAL	PALATE
Robust and herbal, barrel-forward but balanced. It does well with water though it doesn't need it either. The port influence is clear but integrated.	Lots of dill, mint, burnt orange, vegetal, baking chocolate
	PRICE **RATING**
	$$

Deadwood

Deadwood is one of several rye whiskeys created by Dave Schmier after he struck it rich with his first whiskey venture, Redemption, managing to rapidly grow the brand of sourced bourbon and rye during the early days of the craft boom. Deadwood carries no age statement but it is bottled young, to reflect what Schmier considers a historic "frontier" style of rye whiskey.

Deadwood Rye

A blend of two ryes, one with 95 percent rye and 5 percent malted barley, the other 70 percent rye, 13 percent corn, and 12 percent malted barley

AGE
No age statement

ALC/VOL
41.5%

NOSE	MOUTHFEEL	FINISH
Apple butter, celery, sesame, peanut	Full	Short; pumpkin spice

GENERAL	PALATE		
It has the bones of a good whiskey, but it's thin and probably too low in proof to show much meat.	Orange zest, vanilla, celery, dill		
	PRICE	RATING	
	$	★ ★	

Devils River Whiskey

SAN ANTONIO, TEXAS

Devils River Whiskey takes its name from a tributary flowing into the Rio Grande about three hours east of San Antonio. Its founder, Mike Cameron, started making spirits at Rebecca Creek, another San Antonio distillery, before going off on his own to focus on producing whiskey. In 2020 Devils River opened a new distillery near downtown San Antonio, which includes a proprietary system for recycling the thousands of gallons of water that the facility expects to use each day.

Devils River Rye

51 percent rye, 45 percent corn, and 4 percent malted barley

AGE	No age statement	
ALC/VOL	**45**%	
NOSE Cheerios, brown sugar, vanilla cream, lemon, burlap, grass	**MOUTHFEEL** Light	**FINISH** Short; menthol
GENERAL Classic rye flavor profile; young and simple but headed in the right direction.	**PALATE** Lemon cake, grain, menthol, mushroom, almond shells	
PRICE $$	**RATING** ★★	

Distillery 291

DENVER, COLORADO

Michael Myers left behind a career in New York fashion and photography when he moved out to Colorado and opened Distillery 291 in 2011—his first still was constructed from his old copper photogravure plates, like those used to produce photographs in the nineteenth century. The company has grown rapidly thanks to a string of awards and recognitions, including "world's best rye" from Whisky Magazine in 2018. The distillery also makes bourbon, unaged spirit, and American whiskey, as well as something it calls "Colorado whiskey," with a unique mash bill.

Distillery 291 Colorado Rye

61 percent rye and 39 percent corn; finished on aspen staves

AGE		
No age statement		
ALC/VOL		
50%		

NOSE	MOUTHFEEL	FINISH
Cherries, turbinado sugar, cloves, dried mint	Light to medium	Long; cocoa and chalk

GENERAL	PALATE	
A weird and wild whiskey, full of unexpected and challenging notes. You could teach a seminar about this rye.	Lots of dill, mint, burnt orange, vegetal, baking chocolate	

PRICE	RATING
$$$	

Doc Swinson's Whiskey

NO LOCATION

Doc Swinson's is part of a growing group of what are often called "merchant bottlers": brands that buy whiskey from distilleries, then age, blend, finish, and bottle it themselves. Though Doc Swinson's offers the occasional single-barrel release, its strength is blending and finishing. Its rye whiskey is sourced from MGP and placed in ex-rum casks; a portion is then drawn off to bottle, and new whiskey is added—a process adapted from the solera method used in Spain to make sherry.

Doc Swinson's Alter Ego Solera Method Rye Finished in Rum Casks

Undisclosed mash bill

AGE No age statement		
ALC/VOL **47.5**%		
NOSE Apples, plums, lemon, hay, almond oil, dill	**MOUTHFEEL** Medium	**FINISH** Medium; cardboard
GENERAL Great nose and palate, but it falls apart as it moves to the finish.	**PALATE** Milk chocolate, salted caramel, lemon, dill	
	PRICE $$	**RATING** ★★

Driftless Glen Distillery

BARABOO, WISCONSIN

During the last Ice Age, glaciers flattened much of the upper Midwest, leaving behind boulders and deep sediment deposits, also known as drift. The Driftless Area is an anomaly: Sitting at the intersection of Wisconsin, Iowa, Minnesota, and Illinois, it went uncovered by glaciers, and so boasts rolling hills, steep gorges, and verdant river valleys. Driftless Glen, which sits on the Baraboo River northwest of Madison, takes advantage of this unique geological history, drawing on grain raised in its sandy soil and water filtered through nearby peat bogs. Despite its small size and rural location, it has been impressing judges and attracting fans with its rye and bourbon for years.

Driftless Glen Small Batch Straight Rye Whiskey

75 percent rye and 25 percent malted barley

AGE	No age statement
ALC/VOL	**48**%

NOSE	MOUTHFEEL	FINISH
Apples, plums, lemon, hay, almond oil, dill	Medium	Medium; cardboard

GENERAL	PALATE
Great nose and palate, but it falls apart as it moves to the finish.	Milk chocolate, salted caramel, lemon, dill

PRICE	RATING
$$	

Duke Spirits

NO LOCATION

John Wayne, the Hollywood film star known as The Duke, was said to like a good drink, and his son Ethan set out to honor him with a line of bourbon and rye. According to the brand, the whiskey is blended in keeping with a recipe that Wayne left behind after his death in 1972, alongside a stash of his favorite bottles.

Duke Double Barrel Founder's Reserve Rye

Undisclosed mash bill

AGE		
No age statement		

ALC/VOL		
49%		

NOSE	MOUTHFEEL	FINISH
Brown sugar, coffee liqueur, roasted walnuts, tart, banana cream	Medium to full	Medium; cocoa

GENERAL	PALATE	
Two very different flavor profiles struggle here—warm, nutty, salty, buttery, and sunny fights with blueberry, solvent, cocoa, and young crafty flavors. In the end, they don't balance, but they do please.	Milk chocolate, salted caramel, lemon, dill	

PRICE	RATING
$$$$	

E.H. Taylor Whiskey

FRANKFORT, KENTUCKY

Col. Edmund H. Taylor Jr. was one of the original bourbon barons, responsible not only for what became the Buffalo Trace distillery and the Old Taylor distillery, but for many of the basic principles behind modern bourbon marketing. In his honor, Buffalo Trace created a line of premium whiskeys in his name. After sitting on shelves for a few years, they began to take off among fans in the late 2010s, and are now among the most coveted bourbons and ryes in Kentucky.

Colonel E.H. Taylor Straight Rye Bottled in Bond

Undisclosed mash bill, but exclusively rye and malted barley, unlike the standard Buffalo Trace rye mash bill

AGE	ALC/VOL
No age statement	**50**%

NOSE	MOUTHFEEL	FINISH
Cheddar popcorn, dill, hay, raspberry	Medium	Medium; bitter

GENERAL	PALATE
A decent set of flavors, without enough amplitude or progressions to be fascinating.	Aspirin, mint, orange cream, candied citrus

PRICE	RATING
$$$	

Eleven Wells Distillery

ST. PAUL, MINNESOTA

Nothing if not transparent, 11 Wells includes a geekily thorough amount of information on every bottle, detailing production process, dates, and grain source, among many other data points. Such level of information allows drinkers to follow the distillery as it makes changes to its recipe, distillation, and aging. One thing that doesn't change is the water: The distillery sits in a former brewery located above a series of natural wells, which provide all the water it needs— hence the name.

11 Wells Prototype Rye

90 percent rye and 10 percent malted rye

AGE	No age statement	
ALC/VOL	**42**%	

NOSE	MOUTHFEEL	FINISH
Toasted grain, fenugreek, sawdust, burlap	Thin	Lingering grain

GENERAL	PALATE	
Youthfully herbal, with loads of grain notes. It is a well-made whiskey but it needs more age to tone down the overbearing graininess.	Milk chocolate, salted caramel, lemon, dill	

PRICE	RATING
$$	★ ★

Elijah Craig

BARDSTOWN, KENTUCKY

Distilled and aged by Heaven Hill, this whiskey is an homage to Elijah Craig, a real person with a mythical past. He was a Virginia preacher who moved west into what is now Kentucky in the late eighteenth century, and like many white settlers, took up distilling. According to lore but not fact, he invented bourbon whiskey. He didn't—no one did—but his name is revered enough for Heaven Hill to put it on one of its most successful lines of bourbon and rye.

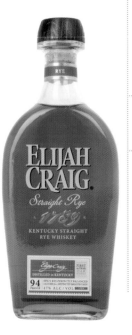

Elijah Craig Straight Rye

51 percent rye, 37 percent corn, and 12 percent malted barley

AGE	No age statement
ALC/VOL	**47**%

NOSE	MOUTHFEEL	FINISH
Peanut shells, aspirin, baking spices, white pepper	Light	Short; minty

GENERAL	PALATE
The nose is very weak, but the palate is pleasantly conventional rye.	Roasted nuts, cocoa powder, honey, dill

PRICE	RATING
$$	

Ezra Brooks

BARDSTOWN, KENTUCKY

Ezra Brooks is a flagship brand of Lux Row, a stately new distillery that sits at the end of a tree-lined road, atop a fielded hill on the outskirts of Bardstown, Kentucky. The sizable distillery and rows of hulking black warehouses will be a shock to someone more familiar with its former parent company, Luxco, which for decades bought whiskey in bulk from other distilleries. When those sources started to dry up, Luxco decided to invest in its own production. These days Lux Row, and Luxco, are owned by MGP Ingredients, best known for its own enormous distillery in Indiana.

Ezra Brooks Straight Rye

51 percent rye, 45 percent corn, and 4 percent malted barley

AGE 2 years old		
ALC/VOL 45%		
NOSE Honeysuckle, honey-roasted peanuts, burdock root	**MOUTHFEEL** Light	**FINISH** Creamy mint, chocolate, and peanuts
GENERAL Immature and unbalanced, though the finish almost redeems it.	**PALATE** Milk chocolate, salted caramel, lemon, dill	
	PRICE $$	**RATING** ★★

Far North Spirits

HALLOCK, MINNESOTA

Far North's motto is "drinking is an agricultural act." Located near the Minnesota-Canada border, the distillery is truly farm-to-glass, drawing on the 1,000 acres of pitch-black soil owned for more than 100 years by the family of Michael Swanson and Cheri Reese, Far North's founders. Though they make gin and other whiskey styles, rye takes pride of place at Far North. In the 2010s the distillery undertook a multi-year research project with the state's department of agriculture to see whether a rye whiskey's flavor varied depending on the grain. They planted dozens of rye varietals around the farm, then distilled and aged each into whiskey. The results were definitive—different varietals produced different flavors, a discovery that opens the door for innovative distilleries everywhere.

Far North Roknar Rye

80 percent rye, 10 percent corn, and 10 percent malted barley

AGE	16 months
ALC/VOL	**47**%

NOSE	MOUTHFEEL	FINISH
Butterscotch, varnish, new leather, sherry	Full	Medium; licorice and spice

GENERAL	PALATE
Aggressive on the nose, aggressive on the palate. It's not unenjoyable, but it needs to chill out.	Mushroom broth, Cognac, mint, dill
	PRICE **$$**
	RATING ★★

F.E.W. Spirits

EVANSTON, ILLINOIS

Evanston, just north of Chicago, was both a hotspot for distilling before Prohibition and the birthplace of one of the Temperance movement's most impassioned leaders,

Frances Elizabeth Willard. Almost a century after the Eighteenth Amendment banned the production and sale of potable alcohol, a lawyer named Paul Hletko decided to revive the city's past liquid glory—and honor Willard by using her initials as his new distillery's name. Along with rye, F.E.W. makes a wide variety of whiskeys and other spirits, and is known for its playful innovations, like cutting some of its whiskeys with cold brew coffee or tea.

F.E.W. Straight Rye

70 percent rye, 20 percent corn, and 10 percent malted barley

AGE	ALC/VOL
No age statement	**46.5**%

NOSE	MOUTHFEEL	FINISH
Cucumber, mint, dill, linen, marigold	Light to medium	Espresso bean, bitters

GENERAL	PALATE
A little unconventional, but the chocolate-mint flavors suggest balance between the grain and barrel.	Malt, mint, chocolate-chewy, and sweetly herbal

PRICE	RATING
$$	★★

F.E.W. Immortal Rye

70 percent rye, 20 percent corn, and 10 percent malted barley; proofed with oolong tea

AGE	ALC/VOL
No age statement	**46.5**%

NOSE	MOUTHFEEL	FINISH
Grain silo, cedar, cola, furniture polish, leather	Full	Short; herbal

GENERAL	PALATE
A youthful, assertive rye, with dry, zesty flavors and a round, slightly oily mouthfeel.	Cola, peppermint, oregano, black pepper, herbal iced tea

PRICE	RATING
$$	★★★

Filibuster Distillery

MAURERTOWN, VIRGINIA

Filibuster began as a sourced brand produced by the Dilawri family, who owned a liquor store near Capitol Hill in Washington, D.C. Like many leading NDPs, they focused on blending and finishing, at a time—2013—when both concepts were still poorly understood by anyone except hardcore whiskey fans. Filibuster soon proved so successful that the family decided to take the leap into distilling, converting a former apple processing plant about an hour west of the city in the Shenandoah Valley into a distillery and tasting room.

Filibuster Dual Cask Rye

90 percent rye and 10 percent malted barley; finished in French oak ex-wine casks

AGE	No age statement
ALC/VOL	**45**%

NOSE	MOUTHFEEL	FINISH
Acetone, eucalyptus, apple candy, peanut shells	Medium	Short; dull and oak-heavy

GENERAL	PALATE
Young, flat, and flabby. Don't add water.	Medicinal and herbal, with some strong oak and rye spice at mid-palate

PRICE	RATING
$$	★★

Fort Hamilton Distillery

BROOKLYN, NEW YORK

Alex Clark always wanted to start his own whiskey operation. After working as bartender and distiller at Brooklyn's Widow Jane, he set off on his own in 2017 with Fort Hamilton, named for a Revolutionary War military installation in southern Brooklyn. He started by contract distilling as a facility upstate, then opened his own distillery and tasting room in Industry City, a former warehouse complex turned shopping and nightlife district on the borough's waterfront.

Fort Hamilton Private Barrel Cask Strength Rye

90 percent rye and 10 percent malted barley

AGE	
4 years old	

ALC/VOL
58.5%

NOSE	MOUTHFEEL	FINISH
Light tobacco, dill seed, lilac, sherry	Light to medium	Medium; pepper

GENERAL	PALATE
This is a fun whiskey. A lot of funky notes going on, but they're not terribly pronounced and all seem roped together nicely.	Cola, peppermint, oregano, black pepper, herbal iced tea

PRICE	RATING
$$$	★★★

Fort Hamilton Double Barrel Rye

Blend of house-distilled and MGP whiskey

AGE
No age statement

ALC/VOL
46%

NOSE	MOUTHFEEL	FINISH
Reticent, with pine, mint, and Lemon Pledge	Medium	Long; minty tingle

GENERAL	PALATE
It's a pleasant enough whiskey but lacks a nose, though more importantly it lacks depth. It's all delicate top notes.	Floral, mint, papaya, lemon pith, malt

PRICE	RATING
$$	★★

Four Gate Whiskey Co.

LOUISVILLE, KENTUCKY

They say you never step in the same river twice; the same could be said of drinking Four Gate. Each of its very limited-release batches is unique, from component whiskies and blend proportions to the custom-made barrels from Kelvin Cooperage, a maker of bespoke casks in downtown Louisville. Four Gate releases several batches a year, both bourbon and rye, and all of them sell out quickly.

Four Gate River Kelvin Rye

BATCH 7

95 percent rye and 5 percent malted barley

AGE
No age statement

ALC/VOL
56.6%

NOSE
Bright lemon, fresh laundry, ginger, cherry syrup

MOUTHFEEL
Full

FINISH
Long; spicy

GENERAL
A robust, chewy, mature rye that takes water well but doesn't need it to blossom.

PALATE
Clove, allspice, cinnamon, ginger, chocolate, almonds

PRICE
$$$$

RATING

Frey Ranch Distillery

FALLON, NEVADA

Located near Lake Tahoe, Frey Ranch is truly farm-to-glass: Everything in its whiskey, from the grains to the water, comes from the 2,000-acre Frey family farm. Like several other young Western farmers, Colby and Ashley Frey realized that they could diversify the farm's output by turning some of its crops into whiskey. They started playing around with distilling in the mid-2000s, and opened the distillery in 2014. Because the farm already provided a steady income, the Freys could afford to wait until they had a 4-year-old product they liked, and even now Frey whiskeys are hard to find outside of a few states.

Frey Ranch Bottled-in-Bond Rye

100 percent rye

AGE No age statement		
ALC/VOL **50**%		
NOSE Tinned tomato, raw grain, astringent, musky, iron, dill	**MOUTHFEEL** Medium	**FINISH** Medium; sweet and spicy
GENERAL Somewhat of an oddball and maybe not for everyone, but this is a whiskey with a point of view and it's proud of it.	**PALATE** Malt, chocolate, roasted nuts, cinnamon candy, butterscotch	
	PRICE **$$$**	**RATING** ★★

George Dickel Whiskey

TULLAHOMA, TENNESSEE

George Dickel may pale in size compared to Jack Daniel's, another stalwart Tennessee brand, but its reputation is just as strong. Especially these days: Nicole Austin, who took over production in 2018, has revitalized the once-sleepy Cascade Hollow Distillery, where Dickel is made, pushing out a steady variety of new and exciting releases, and winning awards— *Whisky Advocate* magazine named George Dickel Bottled-in-Bond its whiskey of the year in 2019, and included Dickel 8-Year-Old Bourbon on its annual roundup of the top 20 best whiskies of the year in 2021. Oddly, although the distillery has produced rye for years, George Dickel Rye is sourced from MGP; the house-made juice appears in dozens of non-distilling producer brands, immediately recognizable by its red apple and cinnamon candy notes.

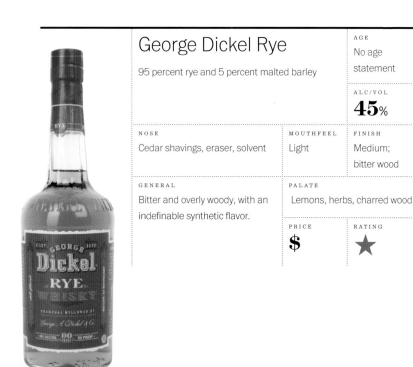

George Dickel Rye

95 percent rye and 5 percent malted barley

AGE No age statement		
ALC/VOL **45**%		

NOSE	MOUTHFEEL	FINISH
Cedar shavings, eraser, solvent	Light	Medium; bitter wood

GENERAL	PALATE	
Bitter and overly woody, with an indefinable synthetic flavor.	Lemons, herbs, charred wood	
	PRICE $	**RATING** ★

Grand Traverse Distillery

TRAVERSE CITY, MICHIGAN

Grand Traverse is a family affair: Founder Kent Rabish runs the business side, his son Landis oversees the distilling, and another son, Steve, manages the logistics. The distillery gets all its grain from another family, the Sends, whose farm sits about 10 miles away. The Rabishes trace their whiskey history to Kent's grandfather, an alleged moonshiner whose still Kent found as a boy, sitting in a seemingly abandoned barn. Grand Traverse has been in operation since 2005, making it one of the country's oldest craft distilleries.

Ole George Double Barrel Rye

100 percent rye and finished in toasted French white oak barrels

AGE		
No age statement		
ALC/VOL		
46.5%		

NOSE	MOUTHFEEL	FINISH
Grape fruit leather, tart cherries, herbal honey, potpourri	Medium	Lengthy; mint tea

GENERAL	PALATE
Simple, straightforward, but more complex than its age might anticipate.	Tobacco, dill, cacao nibs, black tea, mint

PRICE	RATING
$$$	★★ ✦

Ole George Straight Rye

100 percent rye

AGE		
No age statement		
ALC/VOL		
46.5%		

NOSE	MOUTHFEEL	FINISH
Grape candy, leather, pencil shavings, grain, cocoa	Medium	Medium; coffee

GENERAL	PALATE
Dark and roasted, with an intense youthfulness that's not for everyone.	Cinnamon, grape candy, celery, herbal, mint tea

PRICE	RATING
$$$	★★

Hard Truth Distilling

NASHVILLE, INDIANA

Located about an hour south of Indianapolis, Hard Truth is one of the state's fastest-growing distilleries. What started in 2015 as a tiny setup above a pizza parlor quickly became an 18,000-square-foot operation, set into a 325-acre location that also features a restaurant, hiking trails, and ATV tracks. Along with whiskey, Hard Truth makes vodka, gin, and coconut rum. Its rye whiskey, aside from the sweet mash, is sourced.

Hard Truth Indiana Straight Rye

Undisclosed mash bill

AGE		
No age statement		

ALC/VOL
50%

NOSE	MOUTHFEEL	FINISH
Orange drink, peanuts, tobacco, linen, dried fruit	Full	Medium; raisin

GENERAL	PALATE
An engaging, herbaceous rye that blooms with a few drops of water.	Creamy, white chocolate, fruit chews, dried fruit, slate

PRICE	RATING
$$	

Hard Truth Sweet Mash Straight Rye

Undisclosed mash bill

AGE	ALC/VOL
No age statement	**47.6**%

NOSE	MOUTHFEEL	FINISH
Vanilla, cream, nutmeg, unfinished wood	Medium to full	Medium; spicy

GENERAL	PALATE
The nose is shy, but the palate is dessert in a glass. A very enjoyable whiskey.	Vanilla, heavy cream, marzipan, spicy white chocolate

PRICE	RATING
$$$	

Henry A. Sipes' Barrel Smoked Straight Rye

Undisclosed mash bill; finished in hardwood-smoked barrels

AGE	ALC/VOL
4 years old	**45**%

NOSE	MOUTHFEEL	FINISH
Pomegranate, tomato, molasses, rose hips	Medium	Long; tart berries

GENERAL	PALATE
It is sophisticated and interesting, but those qualities obscure the rye itself. Still, its complexity makes it worth taking time to unpack.	Wood spice, fruit leather, herbal, honey glaze

PRICE	RATING
$$	

Heaven's Door Whiskey

NASHVILLE, TENNESSEE

Heaven's Door is the brainchild of entrepreneur Marc Bushala and musician Bob Dylan. There are many, many celebrity spirits on the market, but—despite the fact that Dylan has never given a public interview about the whiskey nor been seen drinking it—Heaven's Door insists that Dylan is an integral part of production, vetting whiskey and offering tasting notes. The company began by sourcing its whiskey, with plans to open a distillery in downtown Nashville to make some of its spirits. Along with its three regular-release expressions, Heaven's Door also offers an annual Bootleg series, a limited run of rare whiskey packaged in bottles featuring some of Dylan's artwork.

Heaven's Door Straight Rye

95 percent rye and 5 percent malted barley

AGE	
7 years old	

ALC/VOL 46%

NOSE	MOUTHFEEL	FINISH
Peanut shell, toasted grain, linseed oil, nutmeg	Light	Short and hot

GENERAL	PALATE
The nose promises more than the palate can deliver, but it's not an offensive dram by any means.	Juicy Fruit, apples, pears, cinnamon, caramel

PRICE	RATING
$$$	

High Plains Whiskey

NO LOCATION

Jim Rutledge is a Kentucky legend. He spent nearly fifty years at Four Roses, much of it during the era when the distillery's domestic whiskey was a bottom-shelf blend and all the good stuff got exported. Rutledge played a critical part in persuading Kirin, the Japanese beverage company that bought the distillery, to invest in its plant and to boost Four Roses's domestic standing. By the time he left in 2015, Four Roses was an icon once more. But Rutledge didn't retire: Today he consults for other brands and distilleries, while putting out his own stock in anticipation of launching his own distillery.

High Plains Rye

A blend of five straight rye mash bills

AGE	
No age statement	

ALC/VOL
48.5%

NOSE	MOUTHFEEL	FINISH
Mint, dill, grain, geranium, cucumber, celery	Light	Short; bitter

GENERAL	PALATE	
A youthful, down-the-line rye, balanced, but thin and uncomplex, and lacking intensity.	Chocolate, mint, grain, celery, herbaceous, apricot	

PRICE	RATING
$$$	★★

High West Distillery

PARK CITY, UTAH

High West is both a distillery and a non-distilling producer.
It buys the bulk of its whiskey from other distilleries, then
ages, blends, and finishes it in-house. But the company also
operates two distilleries of its own, in Park City and Wanship,
Utah, which offer another stream of whiskey for the blending
operation. The formula is getting something right: In 2016
Whisky Advocate named High West "Distiller of the Year," and
in 2017 Constellation Brands, a wine and spirits company,
bought the distillery for an estimated $160 million.

High West Double Rye!

A blend of 95 percent rye and 5 percent malted
barley whiskey from MGP and 80 percent rye and
20 percent malted rye whiskey from High West

AGE
No age
statement

ALC/VOL
46%

NOSE	MOUTHFEEL	FINISH
Cherry candy, honey, almond paste, grape soda, iron	Light to medium	Short; Creamsicle

GENERAL	PALATE
Unremarkable and reticent. It lacks an edge, or character of any sort.	Clove, cinnamon, then white pepper burn, grape candy

PRICE
$$

RATING

High West A Midwinter's Night's Dram ACT 6 SCENE 3

A blend of 95 percent rye and 5 percent malted barley whiskey from MGP and 80 percent rye and 20 percent malted rye whiskey from High West; finished in port and French oak casks

AGE No age statement		
ALC/VOL **49.3**%		

NOSE	MOUTHFEEL	FINISH
Molasses, cherries, apricots, prunes, cinnamon	Medium to full	Lingering sweetness

GENERAL	PALATE
The port influence is clear, present, and at times overwhelming. But the rye manages to hold its own. Save this one for a holiday dessert.	Prunes, molasses, dried cherries, vanilla, cough syrup

PRICE	RATING
$$$$	★★★★

High West Rendezvous Rye

A blend of 95 percent rye and 5 percent malted barley whiskey from MGP and 80 percent rye and 20 percent malted rye whiskey from High West

AGE No age statement		
ALC/VOL **46**%		

NOSE	MOUTHFEEL	FINISH
Dark fruit, roses, sulfur, grilled orange	Light	Lingering; spicy

GENERAL	PALATE
A well-balanced example of a dark rye profile. It could use a touch of sweetness, but overall it's a solid, enjoyable dram.	Molasses, apricot, baking spices, ginger, prunes, somewhat dry

PRICE	RATING
$$	★★½

High Wire Distilling

CHARLESTON, SOUTH CAROLINA

Few distilleries have invested as much in local, heirloom distillation as High Wire. Located in downtown Charleston, High Wire puts the Low Country in every bottle, from its version of a rhum agricole, made from cane stands tucked away on nearby farms, to amaro made with local herbs, to bourbon made with heritage Jimmy Red corn, a varietal found almost exclusively along the Carolina coast. Scott Blackwell and Ann Marshall, the husband-and-wife team behind the distillery, are constantly turning out innovative and limited-release spirits, so if you're in Charleston, it's worth stopping by for a visit.

High Wire New Southern Revival Rye

100 percent rye

AGE		
No age statement		

ALC/VOL		
45%		

NOSE	MOUTHFEEL	FINISH
Floral, lightly herbal, gummy bears, apricots	Medium	Medium; mint and chocolate

GENERAL	PALATE	
A conventional rye, on the light and airy side—a solid candidate for a summer sipper.	Candied violets, orange peel, dill, powdered sugar	

PRICE	RATING
$$$	

Hillrock Estate Distillery

ANCRAM, NEW YORK

Hillrock Estate was among the signature projects of Dave Pickerell, the former master distiller at Maker's Mark who went on to a legendary career as a whiskey consultant, helping dozens of craft startups find their way. Hillrock was one of his first clients, and among the most successful: Located in the Hudson Valley, it was designed from the get-go to be largely field-to-glass, drawing on an expansive farm to supply its grain. The distillery malts its own barley and runs its spirit through a traditional copper pot still.

Hillrock Estate Double Cask Rye

100 percent rye

AGE		
No age statement		

ALC/VOL		
45%		

NOSE	MOUTHFEEL	FINISH
Solvent, putty, new sneaker, blackberry jam	Full	Bittersweet chocolate, mint; lingers

GENERAL	PALATE	
It tastes young but interesting; it's idiosyncratic but also a good example of today's craft ryes.	Dark chocolate, nuts, smoke, cherry	

PRICE	RATING
$$$	

Hochstadter's

Robert J. Cooper made his name and fortune with St-Germain, an elderflower liqueur that quickly became a mainstay at cocktail bars around the world—some call it the "bartender's ketchup." Cooper knew what he was doing; his family-owned Charles Jacquin et Cie., a Philadelphia-based liqueur maker. On the basis of St-Germain's success, Cooper ventured into whiskey, buying barrels to create Hochstadter's, the country's first "vatted" whiskey—i.e., different barrels are blended and allowed to mellow before bottling. Cooper died unexpectedly in 2017, but the company continues.

Hochstadter's Vatted Straight Rye

A blend of several rye whiskey mashbills

AGE	ALC/VOL
No age statement	**50**%

NOSE	MOUTHFEEL	FINISH
Orange peel, cinnamon, Luxardo cherry, mulling spices	Medium	Long and spicy

GENERAL	PALATE
An expertly constructed whiskey that shows how a proper vatting program can achieve something greater than the sum of its inputs.	Dried red apple, clove, vanilla, brown sugar

PRICE	RATING
$$$	

Hudson Whiskey

GARDINER, NEW YORK

Hudson Whiskey, made at the Tuthilltown Distillery near New Paltz, New York, was among the state's first craft whiskey brands. In fact, it was founder Ralph Erenzo who led the push for New York to create a farm distillery license, which gave tax and paperwork reductions to small distilleries that used mostly New York agricultural products in their spirits. Hudson arrived at the right time, in the late 2000s, when craft cocktails and craft whiskey were both ascendant. Erenzo later sold the distillery to William Grant & Sons, the Scottish company behind single malts like Balvenie and Glenfiddich, which continues to produce a portfolio of bourbon, single malt, and rye.

Hudson Do the Rye Thing Straight Rye

95 percent rye and 5 percent malted barley

AGE	ALC/VOL
No age statement	**46**%

NOSE	MOUTHFEEL	FINISH
Drying paint, peppermint patty, green coffee beans, lavender, pastis	Medium	Long; mint and cola

GENERAL	PALATE
A decidedly craft whiskey with a bunch of oddball notes that shouldn't cohere but somehow do.	Mint chocolate, dill, cinnamon, herbal, cola, chocolate cake

PRICE	RATING
$$	★★

Iowa Legendary Rye

CARROLL, IOWA

Iowa Legendary isn't the only distillery in the state to claim roots in bootlegging, or that its recipe was once favored by the gangster Al Capone. Rich Eggers, the founder, says he started making whiskey illegally, and kept doing it until his hooch became so popular that he had to either go legit or get out, lest the authorities catch wind. True? Perhaps. But Iowa Legendary has other things going for it, like getting its rye from nearby farms and even using a locally built still.

Iowa Legendary Red Label Rye

100 percent rye

AGE No age statement		
ALC/VOL **40**%		
NOSE Candy wafers, lemon curd, burlap, wet hay	**MOUTHFEEL** Light	**FINISH** Short; crisp
GENERAL Shy at first, with some off-flavor of fermentation. Then it settles to something a little tastier. Sweet and fruity	**PALATE** Sour cherries, dry sherry, acetone, grassy sweetness	
	PRICE $$	**RATING**

J.W. Kelly & Co.

CHATTANOOGA, TENNESSEE

A sourced whiskey, J.W. Kelly takes its name from an Irish immigrant who arrived soon after the Civil War. Settling in Chattanooga, he became a successful wholesale rectifier, distiller, and saloon owner, popular enough that his brand lived on after his death in 1907, at least until Prohibition. Though his flagship brand was called Deep Spring, it was another, Old Milford, that a trio of entrepreneurs decided to relaunch in 2017.

J.W. Kelly Melrose Rye Finished in an Amarone Cask

65 percent rye, 20 percent malted barley, and 15 percent malted rye, finished in amarone casks

AGE No age statement		
ALC/VOL **46**%		
NOSE Old leather, cocoa, peach, white wine	**MOUTHFEEL** Full	**FINISH** Medium; dry and tannic
GENERAL It's all over the place, but it manages to work despite—or perhaps because of—that tension.	**PALATE** Peach, apricot, grape soda, cantaloupe	
PRICE $$$	**RATING**	

Jack Daniel Distillery

LYNCHBURG, TENNESSEE

Jack Daniel's is one of the bestselling and best-known whiskey brands in the world—not bad for a distillery tucked into an isolated hollow in middle Tennessee. Jack Daniel was a real person: He founded his eponymous distillery after the Civil War, with Nathan "Nearest" Green, a formerly enslaved person, as his first master distiller. The distillery grew slowly until after World War II, when celebrities like Frank Sinatra started appearing with its bottles on their nightclub tables. Jack Daniel's Tennessee whiskey is basically bourbon, with the added step of filtering the unaged spirit through maple charcoal. That's all it made until 2017, when it debuted its rye whiskey, which undergoes the same filtration process, and has since become one of the distillery's bestsellers.

Jack Daniel's Straight Rye

70 percent rye, 18 percent corn, and 12 percent malted barley

AGE	No age statement
ALC/VOL	**45**%

NOSE	MOUTHFEEL	FINISH
Honey, cherry candy, and malt; water brings out dark fruit	Light to medium	Medium, with peppermint, green apple

GENERAL	PALATE
A lovely nose, with hints of Highlands scotch, but it falls apart with water.	Cocoa powder, honeycomb, cherry Jolly Rancher, slightly bitter

PRICE	RATING
$$	

Jack Daniel's Single Barrel Straight Rye

70 percent rye, 18 percent corn, and 12 percent malted barley

AGE
No age statement

ALC/VOL
47%

NOSE
Baked bread, nutmeg, orange peel, pencil shavings, brown sugar

MOUTHFEEL
Light

FINISH
Long; ginger

GENERAL
Chewy but light bodied, with sweet, soft floral notes.

PALATE
Ginger, honey, cinnamon crumb cake, dark chocolate, plum

PRICE
$$$

RATING

James E. Pepper Distillery

LEXINGTON, KENTUCKY

Amir Peay, the founder of James E. Pepper, is a whiskey geek, but he's also a boxing fan. He was a freelance sports writer when he came across a photo of the Black boxer Jack Johnson, who became the heavyweight champion at the height of the Jim Crow era. Behind Johnson was a banner that read "James E. Pepper Whisky: Born with the Republic," promoting a whiskey brand popular at the time. Peay began collecting Pepper memorabilia, and eventually decided to resurrect the brand itself—first as a sourced whiskey, and then as a distillery. He secured and rehabilitated the original Pepper facility, near downtown Lexington, Kentucky, where he makes bourbon, rye, and a variety of experimental releases (though for now much of his whiskey is sourced, that will change as his own stocks mature).

James E. Pepper 1776 Straight Rye

95 percent rye and 5 percent malted barley

AGE	
3 years old	

ALC/VOL	
50%	

NOSE	MOUTHFEEL	FINISH
Vanilla taffy, solvent, mint	Thin-medium	Lengthy; bitter

GENERAL	PALATE
Vivid and intense, with a robust and flavorful palate.	Mint, chocolate, cloves, dried fruits

PRICE	RATING
$$	★★★

James E. Pepper
Old Pepper Single Barrel
Straight Rye BATCH # K02

95 percent rye and 5 percent malted barley

AGE	
7 years old	

ALC/VOL	
58% *Varies*	

NOSE	MOUTHFEEL	FINISH
Burlap, nail polish, green apple candy	Medium-full	Lingering, with dark fruits and bitters
GENERAL	PALATE	
A perfect pick for a winter's dram—warming, rounded, and balanced.	Pine, gingerbread, semisweet chocolate, toasted wood	
	PRICE	RATING
	$$$	

James E. Pepper 1776
Barrel Proof Straight Rye

95 percent rye and 5 percent malted barley

AGE	
No age statement	

ALC/VOL	
57.3% *Varies*	

NOSE	MOUTHFEEL	FINISH
Lemon, menthol, and slight acetone; also bubble gum, flowers, and eucalyptus	Full	Short to medium; sweet
GENERAL	PALATE	
Complex but not complicated; it might be more enjoyable at a somewhat lower proof.	Sweet and sour sauce, sweet hot peppers, cake, fruit, and black tea	
	PRICE	RATING
	$$$	

James Oliver Rye

NO LOCATION

Like many sourced whiskeys, James Oliver is rooted in the story of a moonshiner. In this case, it's James Oliver Turner, who learned the trade as a boy in Mississippi and later took it with him to Oregon, where he worked in shipyards during World War II. His grandson Robert Turner started the brand in 2013, reportedly using whiskey bought from MGP in Indiana.

James Oliver Rye

Undisclosed mash bill

AGE No age statement		
ALC/VOL **50**%		
NOSE Toast, soap, Juicy Fruit, pine, mint, ashtray tobacco, hops	**MOUTHFEEL** Medium	**FINISH** Long; heat
GENERAL Unbalanced with a lot of heat on the palate and finish. The heat dissipates a bit with air, but not entirely.	**PALATE** Herbaceous, apple cider, rubber, clove, black pepper	
	PRICE $$	**RATING**

Jim Beam

CLERMONT, KENTUCKY

With its three distilleries spread around Kentucky, Jim Beam is one of the largest whiskey makers in the world, and it has one of the longest pedigrees, tracing back to Jacob Beam, who arrived in Kentucky in the late eighteenth century and almost immediately began making whiskey. One of his many descendants, Jim Beam, restarted the family business under his own name after Prohibition, and his great-grandson, Fred Noe, currently serves as master distiller. Jim Beam is mostly known as a bourbon distillery, but it has a number of rye expressions, all using its Kentucky-style rye mash bill.

Jim Beam Rye

Undisclosed mash bill

AGE		
No age statement		
ALC/VOL		
40%		

NOSE	MOUTHFEEL	FINISH
Peanut, Cherry Coke, Red Hots, orange peel	Light	Short; leather

GENERAL	PALATE
A delicate whiskey—the nose is quite shy, and water obliterates the palate. But even without water, it's one-dimensional without much follow-through on the palate.	Clove, cherry, orange peel, cinnamon, tobacco

PRICE	RATING
$$$	★

Journeyman Distillery

THREE OAKS, MICHIGAN

Tucked into a renovated buggy-whip and corset factory in southwestern Michigan, Journeyman started making spirits for the Lake Michigan region in the early 2010s, then slowly expanded to national markets over the next decade. Founder Bill Welter trained with Robert Birnecker, the co-founder of Koval Distillery in Chicago, before opening his distillery in 2011. Journeyman's whiskies all pay homage to the facility's location, with names like Featherbone (a type of corset material) and, well, Corsets, Whips & Whiskey.

Journeyman Last Feather Rye

60 percent rye and 40 percent wheat

AGE	
No age statement	
ALC/VOL	
45%	

NOSE	MOUTHFEEL	FINISH
Wet grain, vanilla, simple syrup, acetone	Light	Short with a bit of spice

GENERAL	PALATE
It's more like a grain whiskey, or Canadian, than an American rye.	Almond, honeysuckle, vanilla, beeswax

PRICE	RATING
$$$	★★

Kentucky Owl Whiskey

BARDSTOWN, KENTUCKY

The original Kentucky Owl, founded by C.W. Dedman, was among the state's largest distilleries in the late nineteenth century, but like many, it crashed and disappeared during Prohibition. Dixon Dedman, a descendant of C.W., resurrected the brand in the 2010s with his friends Mark and Sherri Carter, releasing it batch by batch in both bourbon and rye expressions. The partners later sold the brand to Stoli Group, though Dedman stayed on as master blender until 2021.

Kentucky Owl Straight Rye

BATCH NO. 4

Undisclosed mash bill

AGE
10
years old

ALC/VOL
56.4%

NOSE	MOUTHFEEL	FINISH
Butterscotch, wildflowers, straw, leather, tobacco	Full	Long; sweet

GENERAL	PALATE
A nearly perfect rye, achieving a precise balance of tobacco, dessert sweetness, and marzipan, with a well-aged frame almost like an Armagnac.	Vanilla, caramel, marzipan, leather, touch of smoke

PRICE
$$$$

RATING
★★
★★

Kentucky Owl
The Wiseman Rye

Undisclosed mash bill

AGE
No age statement

ALC/VOL
50.4%

NOSE
Lilacs, honey biscuits, fennel, dill

MOUTHFEEL
Medium

FINISH
Lingering spice

GENERAL
A conventional rye profile, but well-structured and enjoyable. Don't expect fireworks, just a solid whiskey.

PALATE
Mint, dill, peppercorn, orange bitters, cinnamon candy

PRICE
$$$

RATING
★★

Kings County Distillery

BROOKLYN, NEW YORK

When it was founded in 2010, Kings County was among the first distilleries in New York City to open since Prohibition, and likewise one of the first to take advantage of the state's farm distillery license, which gives tax breaks to and eases paperwork for small distilleries that use locally sourced ingredients. After a short stint working out of an industrial space, Kings County moved to the landmarked Paymaster building in Brooklyn's Navy Yard complex. Under the direction of distiller and co-founder Colin Spoelman, Kings County has become a perennial award-winner at whiskey competitions nationwide and a favorite of whiskey drinkers, who are drawn as much by its flavor as by its distinctive flask-shaped bottles.

Kings County Empire Straight Rye

80 percent rye and 20 percent malted barley

AGE	**2** years old	
ALC/VOL	**51**%	

NOSE	MOUTHFEEL	FINISH
Celery, apple skins, Calvados, nutty	Medium	Spicy pepper, oregano, and chocolate

GENERAL	PALATE
Balanced and enjoyable; a well-crafted young whiskey that works well at a high proof.	Honey, with a sweet, bready backbone; there's cinnamon and caramel too

PRICE	RATING
$$	

Knob Creek

CLERMONT, KENTUCKY

Jim Beam created Knob Creek in 1992, part of the distillery's push into higher-end whiskey in the earliest days of the bourbon resurgence. Knob Creek is the name of a farm where Abraham Lincoln spent part of his boyhood, located in central Kentucky not too far from Beam's distilleries. Beam added Knob Creek rye to the portfolio in 2012.

Knob Creek Straight Rye

Undisclosed mash bill

AGE	ALC/VOL
No age statement	**50**%

NOSE	MOUTHFEEL	FINISH
Black pepper, linseed oil, attic wood, coffee, cinnamon	Full	Short; spicy

GENERAL	PALATE
A classic Kentucky rye profile, with all the right moves—some spice but not too much; some sweetness but again not too much. It's a utility player, good in cocktails or on its own.	Dark chocolate, roasted nuts, Juicy Fruit, cloves

PRICE	RATING
$$$	★★★

KO Distilling

MANASSAS, VIRGINIA

Located in the suburbs of Washington, D.C., KO Distilling was founded by Bill Karlson and John O'Mara, friends since their cadet days at the U.S. Merchant Marine Academy.

It was only after they retired, however, that they decided to go into the distilling business together. They founded KO—their last initials, but also a catchy name for high-proof spirits—in 2015, and have since released a wide portfolio, including gin, unaged whiskey, and several versions of bourbon and rye.

KO Bareknuckle Straight Rye Whiskey

100 percent rye

AGE No age statement		
ALC/VOL **45**%		
NOSE Maple, slight mint, clove, roasted nuts	**MOUTHFEEL** Full	**FINISH** Short; chocolate
GENERAL A pleasing aroma and palate, but the rye character is muted.	**PALATE** Orange, vanilla, mint, baking spices	
PRICE **$$**	**RATING** ★ ★	

Kooper Family Whiskey Co.

LEDBETTER, TEXAS

Troy and Michelle Kooper started out making whiskey at home, as a hobby. Eventually, they decided to make their passion their career. But instead of starting a distillery, they launched a blending house. Based in La Grange, Texas, about half way between Austin and Houston, Kooper Family buys whiskey from Kentucky distilleries and then ages and blends it into a series of regular and one-off releases. To the Koopers, value comes not from the distillate, but what they do with it: aging it in a variety of oak barrels and working with, not against, the harsh Texas climate.

Kooper Family Rye

A blend of 3-year-old, with a mash bill of 51 percent rye, 36 percent corn, and 13 percent malted barley, and 5-year-old with a 95 percent rye and 5 percent malted barley mash bill

AGE		
No age statement		
ALC/VOL		
45%		

NOSE	MOUTHFEEL	FINISH
Floral, cinnamon, banana flambé, varnish	Light	Short; cacao nibs

GENERAL	PALATE	
Fruity and floral, more than you'd expect from a rye. But it coheres, and it works, which is what matters.	Cake batter, chocolate, malt, Juicy Fruit	
	PRICE	RATING
	$$	

Kooper Family Barrel Reserve Rye

A blend of 4-year-old, with a mash bill of 51 percent rye, 36 percent corn, and 13 percent malted barley, and 6-year-old with a 95 percent rye and 5 percent malted barley mash bill

AGE	
No age statement	
ALC/VOL	
58%	

NOSE	MOUTHFEEL	FINISH
Coffee, pipe tobacco, toffee, coffee cake	Full	Long; chocolate-covered orange

GENERAL	PALATE
A dessert rye if there ever was one: cake, thick fruit flavors, and coffee roastiness. Sip it neat or with a few drops of water.	Pastry basket, dark berries, coffee cake, tobacco
	PRICE
	$$
	RATING

Koval Distillery

CHICAGO, ILLINOIS

Koval was and remains one of the pioneers of the Chicago distilling scene, drawing equally on the Windy City's Central European heritage and its connections to the grain baskets of the Midwest. Founders Robert Birnecker and Sonat Birnecker Hart both come to the craft with doctorate degrees in hand, and they bring an intellectual's approach to distilling, from their embrace of obscure grains like millet to their use of a Kothe still, a precision instrument from Germany renowned as the Mercedes of distillation.

Koval Single Barrel Rye

100 percent rye

AGE	
No age statement	
ALC/VOL	
40%	

NOSE	MOUTHFEEL	FINISH
Brownie crust, dark wood, dried fruit, linseed oil	Light	Lingering, with pine and oak

GENERAL	PALATE	
A youthful rye with compact strength, but water takes away its superpowers.	Caraway seed, pine, lime zest, raisins	
	PRICE	RATING
		★★★

Laws Whiskey House

DENVER, COLORADO

After years of toiling quietly and selling locally, Laws Whiskey House has moved up several notches to become one of Colorado's most exciting craft distilleries, with a national reputation based on its use of locally sourced heritage grains and transparency in its production methods. Its rye grain comes from a family farm in the San Luis Valley, nestled

8,000 feet up in the Rockies, significantly higher than the Denver-based distillery itself. Laws makes a core line of straight, bonded, and cask-strength rye, but be on the lookout for one of its many limited releases, including the occasional cask finish.

Laws San Luis Valley Straight Rye BATCH NO. 12

100 percent rye

AGE		
No age statement		

ALC/VOL		
47.5%		

NOSE	MOUTHFEEL	FINISH
Blueberry jam, hops, cinnamon, acetone, plastic car seat	Full	Medium; grassy

GENERAL	PALATE	
The hops note complements the sweet grassiness of it all, but it could still use more age and complexity to hang it all together.	Sage, lemongrass, hops, cream, dill, mint	

	PRICE	RATING
	$$$	★★

Laws San Luis Valley Bonded Rye

100 percent rye

AGE		
6 years old		

ALC/VOL		
50%		

NOSE	MOUTHFEEL	FINISH
Peanut shells, mint, baking spices, leather, brown sugar	Medium	Medium; citrus

GENERAL	PALATE	
A conventional rye on the nose, but it is craft-like and more interesting on the palate.	Lilac, orange peel, baking spices, brown sugar	

	PRICE	RATING
	$$$	★★⭐

Leopold Bros. Distillery

DENVER, COLORADO

Scott and Todd Leopold are the duo behind Leopold Bros., a highly regarded, adamantly craft distillery founded in Ann Arbor, Michigan and now located in Denver. They are relentlessly innovative, even geeky, with eight stills of varying size and design, including a custom-built three-chamber still, thought to be the only working still of its type anywhere. Leopold Bros. is among the only distilleries in America to have its own malting floor. It gets most of the grains and fruit from local producers, and it uses a low-temperature fermentation that, while longer and less efficient, helps bring out nuances often not found in whiskeys made with more cost-effective techniques.

Leopold Brothers Maryland Style Rye

65 percent rye, 15 percent corn and 20 percent malted barley

AGE	ALC/VOL
No age statement	**43**%

NOSE	MOUTHFEEL	FINISH
Grass, chocolate, celery, dill, confectioners' sugar	Light	Short; bitter

GENERAL	PALATE
A decent, young rye for the nose and the first two-thirds of the palate, but it falls apart toward the end and leaves with a disappointing finish.	Hay, milk chocolate, coconut, lime pith, dill, celery

PRICE	RATING
$$$	★★

Leopold Bros. Three Chamber Rye HOLIDAY EDITION

80 percent Abruzzi rye and 20 percent malted barley, distilled on a three-chamber still

AGE
No age statement

ALC/VOL
50%

NOSE	MOUTHFEEL	FINISH
Pine, grain silo, linen, hoppy	Medium	Medium; tannic

GENERAL	PALATE
Hoppy, grainy, almost like an IPA beer, but there's a simplicity that keeps it from greatness.	Pine, dill, cloves, orange and lemon oils, cinnamon

PRICE	RATING
$$$$	

Liberty Pole Spirits

WASHINGTON, PENNSYLVANIA

Liberty poles—wooden staves topped by a cap—are an ancient symbol of rebellion against oppression, originating in the late Roman republic and coming to America during the early days of the Revolution. Supporters of the rebellion against the British put them in front of their houses, or carried them into battle. The poles made a repeat appearance in the early 1790s, when western Pennsylvania farmers rose up against a whiskey excise tax imposed by the federal government. Like Wigle Whiskey in Pittsburgh, Liberty Pole Spirits, based at Mingo Creek Craft Distillers about an hour south, in Washington, takes its inspiration from the Whiskey Rebellion, and is part of the movement to bring Old Monongahela-style rye whiskey back to life.

Liberty Pole Rye

61 percent rye, 13 percent wheat, 13 percent malted rye, and 13 percent malted barley

AGE
No age statement

ALC/VOL
46%

NOSE
Papaya, wholegrain bread, thyme, lemon zest

MOUTHFEEL
Light to medium

FINISH
Faint; fruit

GENERAL
A young and crafty palate—fruity, slightly herbal; it's nicely done but slightly averse to showing its full colors.

PALATE
Grain silo, tropical fruit, chiles, thyme

PRICE
$$

RATING

Limestone Branch Distillery

LEBANON, KENTUCKY

Limestone Branch's founders, Stephen Beam and his brother Paul, are Kentucky whiskey royalty. Their father's side goes back to Jacob Beam, the first distiller in that renowned family, while their mother was a Dant, once among the most famous names in American whiskey. Partly owned by spirits giant MGP, following its 2021 merge with Luxco, Limestone Branch is small, and decidedly low-tech. The distillery produces just under 500 barrels of whiskey a year on a pot still from Hoga, a Portuguese company that makes traditional, manually operated equipment.

Minor Case Sherry Cask Finished Rye

51 percent rye, 45 percent corn and 4 percent malted barley

AGE	ALC/VOL
2 years old	**45**%

NOSE	MOUTHFEEL	FINISH
Dill, raspberries, dried cherries, burlap	Light to medium	Light to medium

GENERAL	PALATE
An easy-drinking rye, and one that demonstrates the benefits of pairing a young rye's herbaceousness with the rich sweetness of a sherry finish.	Dried apricots, raisins, baking spices, cinnamon, chocolate

PRICE	RATING
$$	

Lock, Stock & Barrel Whiskey

NO LOCATION

Like Hochstadter's Vatted Rye, this whiskey is the brainchild of the late Robert J. Cooper, who first made his name in spirits with the creation of St-Germain elderflower liqueur. For Lock, Stock & Barrel, he sourced rye whiskey from Alberta Distillers, the massive Canadian distillery renowned for its well-aged stocks. Lock, Stock & Barrel has been released at several ages.

Lock, Stock & Barrel 18-Year-Old Straight Rye Whiskey

100 percent rye

AGE	**18** years old
ALC/VOL	**54.5**%

NOSE	MOUTHFEEL	FINISH
Persimmons, cinnamon, tangerine, plums, rye spice	Full	Long and fruity

GENERAL	PALATE
Like a fruitcake in a glass—albeit the best fruitcake you can possibly imagine.	Cardamom, baking spices, orange slices, cinnamon sugar

PRICE	RATING
$$	★★★★

Low Gap Whiskey

UKIAH, CALIFORNIA

Crispin Cain, the founder of Low Gap, doesn't own a still—instead, he makes his whiskey at the Tamar distillery. Before co-founding Tamar, Cain apprenticed at Germain-Robin, a California brandy distillery making Old World–style spirits on Charentais stills. He uses those same methods at Tamar. Cain makes bourbon, wheat whiskey, and rye, though he doesn't make much of it, and what he does sell is quickly snapped up by dedicated fans.

Low Gap Rye

Undisclosed mash bill

AGE
2
years old

ALC/VOL
43.6%

NOSE
Cherry licorice, wax, grappa, papaya

MOUTHFEEL
Light

FINISH
Medium; roasted nuts

GENERAL
It's a cavalcade of interesting flavors that don't quite match. There is an intriguing roasted, smoky note that some people will like.

PALATE
Red Hots, varnish, tons of tropical fruit, smoked nuts

PRICE
$$$

RATING
★★

Mad River Distillers

WAITSFIELD, VERMONT

"Mad River" is so perfect a name for a whiskey brand that it must surely be made up. In fact, the Mad River is a picturesque tributary that runs west of Montpelier, cutting through a valley known for its ski slopes. The distillery embraces its cool-weather aging environment; warm but not hot summers hardly offset deep, snowy winters to produce a milder, rounder whiskey than one might find in more Southern climes.

Mad River Revolution Rye

100 percent rye

AGE	No age statement

ALC/VOL	**46%**

NOSE	MOUTHFEEL	FINISH
Berries, dried cod, lavender, Thin Mint, gingersnap	Medium	Medium; cigar

GENERAL	PALATE
It tastes young and crafty, but well-done for all that. Vividly presented with a full, round mouthfeel.	Coffee, cedar, honey, cacao, mint, chile, dill

PRICE	RATING
$$	

Mammoth Distilling

CENTRAL LAKE, MICHIGAN

With locations all along the northwestern coast of Michigan's lower peninsula, Mammoth is a mainstay of the state's craft spirits and cocktail scene. It is also an innovator. Working with the state government, it has planted demonstration fields of Rosen rye, a long-lost but much-admired varietal. The fields are on South Manitou Island, not far from Traverse

City, and the Mammoth team hopes to have enough rye soon to distill—and to share with other distilleries interested in resurrecting this bit of American agricultural history.

Mammoth Woolly Rye

88 percent Wheeler rye, 10 percent 2-row malted barley, and 2 percent caramel malt

AGE	ALC/VOL
No age statement	**46**%

NOSE	MOUTHFEEL	FINISH
Funk, uncooked wet grain, straw, plywood	Light to medium	Medium; mint

GENERAL	PALATE
The nose is raw, immature, and off-putting, but the palate is strangely compelling, like a weird, unfamiliar Halloween candy you can't stop sucking on.	Herbal candies, raw grain, horehound, molasses, mint

PRICE	RATING
$$$	★★

Mammoth 9-Year-Old Northern Rye

A blend of rye, corn, and barley, aged separately, then blended and further aged in used barrels

AGE	ALC/VOL
9 years old	**49.5**%

NOSE	MOUTHFEEL	FINISH
Dried peach, leather, circus peanuts, pineapple juice	Thin to medium	Long; coconut

GENERAL	PALATE
Showing big tropical notes, it's delicate but a little stiff, like a good push will snap it in half—and, indeed, it breaks down with a few drops of water. But tasty nevertheless.	Pineapple, cedar chips, caramel, allspice

PRICE	RATING
$$$	★★

Masterson's Rye

NO LOCATION

Like a few other whiskeys sold by American companies, Masterson's rye comes from Canada (which, if we were being pedantic, would make it "whisky," not "whiskey"). The source, Alberta Distillers, is a massive operation in Calgary that has been called "Canada's MGP" for its ubiquity and consistent high quality. The brand is owned by Deutsch Family Wine & Spirits, and bottled in California.

Masterson's 10-Year-Old Straight Rye

100 percent rye

AGE	**10** years old
ALC/VOL	**45**%

NOSE	MOUTHFEEL	FINISH
Orange drink, European vanilla, almond, nougat	Medium	Medium; tropical fruit

GENERAL	PALATE
An enchanting nose, but a disappointingly flat palate. Solid without being great.	Vanilla, dill, linseed oil, almond paste, tropical fruit candy

PRICE	RATING
$$$	

McKenzie Whiskey

BURDETT, NEW YORK

McKenzie is the flagship brand of Finger Lakes Distilling, located on the southeastern shore of Seneca Lake in Upstate New York. Finger Lakes was among the first distilleries to take advantage of New York's farm distillery license, which was designed to foster craft distilleries by cutting taxes and red tape for startups that use grains and fruit grown in state. The rye is finished in sherry barrels sourced from Upstate New York wineries.

McKenzie Rye Whiskey

80 percent rye and 20 percent malted barley; finished in sherry barrels

AGE
No age statement

ALC/VOL
45.5%

NOSE
Grass, vanilla, grilled peaches, nutmeg

MOUTHFEEL
Light to medium

FINISH
Medium; creamy

GENERAL
McKenzie has always shown promise with its rye, and recently the distillery has hit its stride. This is a phenomenally crafted, youthfully energetic whiskey.

PALATE
Caramel, cream, fruit leather, dried orange peel

PRICE
$$$

RATING

Michter's Distillery

LOUISVILLE, KENTUCKY

The original Michter's distillery operated in Pennsylvania; it traced its history to the Revolutionary War era and unfortunately went under in the late 1980s. A little over a decade later, Joseph Magliocco, who had sold Michter's as a young liquor-industry executive and now commanded Chatham Imports, resurrected the brand, this time as a Kentucky distillery. At first he bought aged whiskey; he later contract-distilled liquid before finally opening Michter's own operation outside Louisville. (The company also has a demonstration still, once housed at the original Michter's, at its visitors center downtown). Extra-mature barrels, which Michter's occasionally releases, are legendary, fetching four or even five figures a bottle.

Michter's 10-Year-Old Single Barrel Straight Rye
2019 RELEASE

Undisclosed mash bill

AGE **10** years old		
ALC/VOL **46.4**%		

NOSE	MOUTHFEEL	FINISH
Balsamic vinegar, light red wine, stone fruits	Full	Lingering cinnamon, mint, white pepper

GENERAL	PALATE
A big, expressive rye, with some complexity but no confusion about what it's trying to do.	Candied fruits, dried ginger, mint

PRICE	RATING
$$$$	★ ★ ★ ★

Michter's US*1 Barrel Strength Straight Rye

Undisclosed mash bill

AGE		
No age statement		

ALC/VOL		
53.5–56%		

NOSE	MOUTHFEEL	FINISH
Hay, cola syrup, roses, tobacco barn	Full	Long; herbal bitters

GENERAL	PALATE	
Big and expressive but balanced and even quaffable. Classic herbal rye flavors with plenty of complexity to keep you interested.	Cola, mint, ginger, pecan pie, chocolate	

PRICE	RATING
$$$$	

Michters US*1 Straight Rye

Undisclosed mash bill

AGE		
No age statement		

ALC/VOL		
42.4%		

NOSE	MOUTHFEEL	FINISH
Stewed plums, pie pastry, blueberries, butterscotch, pumpkin spice	Medium	Medium; bittersweet chocolate

GENERAL	PALATE	
Like holidays in a glass, or a kitchen on Thanksgiving morning. Not a great whiskey, but it's mouth- and crowd-pleasing.	Flat cola, clove, mace, allspice, cardamom, orange peel, fruit tea	

PRICE	RATING
$$	

Michter's Toasted Barrel Finish Rye

Undisclosed mash bill

AGE		No age statement
ALC/VOL		**55**%

NOSE	MOUTHFEEL	FINISH
Cellar mustiness, dried apricots, cedar, pine needles	Full	Medium; tobacco

GENERAL	PALATE
The palate is dry and woodsy yet also somehow not austere—it's loaded with fruit and spice notes.	Orange peel, brown sugar, raisins, tobacco

PRICE	RATING
$$$$	★★ ★↗

Michter's 25-Year-Old Single Barrel Straight Rye

BARREL NO 14L719

Undisclosed mash bill

AGE		**25** years old
ALC/VOL		**58.5**%

NOSE	MOUTHFEEL	FINISH
Lavender, balsamic vinegar, perfume, mushrooms, plum pudding	Full	Long; chocolate raisins

GENERAL	PALATE
This whiskey has it all, literally—just about every note you'd look for in a rye is here, plus so much more. Drawn from barrels distilled in the whiskey "Dark Ages," it has flavors and a complexity that will never be replicated.	Miso, raisins, mushrooms, raspberry, prunes

PRICE	RATING
$$$$	★★ ★★

Middle West Spirits

COLUMBUS, OHIO

Ohio was once among the leading whiskey-distilling states in America, with distilleries lining the Ohio River and its tributaries. That time is long gone, but there are now a few craft outfits trying to bring back the glory. Middle West Spirits, in business since 2008 and distilling since 2010, is chief among them. Its bestselling spirit is OYO Vodka, which pays the bills, but the distillery's heart is clearly in whiskey; along with rye it makes bourbon and wheat whiskey, plus a variety of wine-cask finishes.

Middle West Dark Pumpernickel Straight Rye

Percentages undisclosed, but it contains rye, wheat, corn, and malted barley

AGE		
No age statement		
ALC/VOL		
48%		

NOSE	MOUTHFEEL	FINISH
Powdered grape drink, perfume, butyric funk	Light to medium	Medium; copper

GENERAL	PALATE	
Off-balance and unfinished; it struggles to right itself on the palate and barely manages, but the finish is a new disappointment.	Caramel, cream, fruit leather, dried orange peel	

	PRICE	RATING
	$$	**NR**

Milam & Greene Whiskey

BLANCO, TEXAS

Milam & Greene was founded by three women: entrepreneur Marsha Milam, master blender Heather Greene, and veteran master distiller Marlene Holmes. Each brought their own skill set to the equation, and the result has been one of the most heralded whiskeys to come out of Texas in recent years. Like other distilleries in the Texas Hill Country, Milam & Greene takes advantage of the region's hot summers and mild winters to produce robust, flavorful whiskeys—some of which are sourced—including its flagship bourbon, rye, and a number of distillery-only releases.

Milam & Greene Port Finished Rye

95 percent rye and 5 percent malted barley

AGE		
No age statement		
ALC/VOL		
47%		

NOSE	MOUTHFEEL	FINISH
Red Hots, blackberry, pancake batter, cloves	Light	Long; bitter

GENERAL	PALATE
An interesting mix of flavor notes, but somehow not lovely in combination. Still, it's distinctive and interesting.	Vanilla cream; peppermint; tobacco, overripe fruit

PRICE	RATING
$$	

Mississippi River Distilling Co.

LECLAIRE, IOWA

LeClaire, Iowa sits on the Mississippi River, just upstream from the Quad Cities. A small town, its greatest claim to fame is as the birthplace of Buffalo Bill Cody, whose name adorns roads, cafes, a school—and the whiskeys produced by Mississippi River Distilling. Located on the north side of downtown, the distillery has been making whiskey since 2010, using grains drawn from within a 25-mile radius.

Mississippi River Distilling Cody Road Rye

100 percent rye

AGE	No age statement
ALC/VOL	**48**%

NOSE	MOUTHFEEL	FINISH
Cherry, rose, oregano, cocoa powder, plum, dill, grass	Light	Long; mint

GENERAL	PALATE	
Decent, simple—the nose is refreshing, but the palate is pedestrian. Use it as a mixer.	Toasted grain, cocoa powder, lavender, tomato	

PRICE	RATING
$	

Nashville Barrel Co.

NASHVILLE, TENNESSEE

Like Barrell Craft Spirits, Pinhook, and a growing number of other companies, Nashville Barrel Co. doesn't hide the fact that it sources its whiskey. The three friends behind it—Mike Hinds, James Davenport, and Johnny Tsunami—started as hobbyists, picking barrels for themselves. Eventually they saw the chance to turn their skills into a business, picking and blending whiskeys to bottle in limited releases. Their first offering, a rye, sold out almost overnight; since then they've expanded to offer bourbon and rum as well.

Nashville Barrel Co. Straight Rye   BATCH 1

95 percent rye and 5 percent malted barley

AGE	**4-7** years old
ALC/VOL	**50%**

NOSE	MOUTHFEEL	FINISH
Broth, celery seed, Bloody Mary mix, cake batter	Full	Medium; cola

GENERAL	PALATE
An unusually dry and savory nose and a somewhat lovely sweetness on the opening. Somewhat lacking in vividness, but tasty and interesting.	Honey, cola, cake batter, nutmeg

PRICE	RATING
$$$	★★★

New Basin Distilling Co.

MADRAS, OREGON

Located in Madras, a small town in central Oregon, New Basin has been making whiskey since 2016. Its five founders—a science teacher, a rancher, two farmers, and a crop-duster pilot—not only use mostly locally sourced grains, but they grow a good amount themselves, on a 400-acre farm. The distillery also sources some of its whiskey, a portion of which goes into a line of American light whiskeys.

New Basin Resignation Rye

100 percent rye

AGE 3–4 months old		
ALC/VOL **50**%		
NOSE Nylon, untanned leather, sulfur, mixed herbs	**MOUTHFEEL** Medium	**FINISH** Long; cloves
GENERAL Its youth is apparent, but that's not entirely a drawback—there are interesting, lively flavors here.	**PALATE** Atomic Fireball, grain, artificially floral, earth, mint	
	PRICE **$$**	**RATING**

New England Distilling Co.

PORTLAND, MAINE

Maryland rye was once so popular that people asked for it by name, and among the most popular brands was Sherbrook, made by the Frank L. Wight Distilling Co. The company, brand, and even the very style of Maryland rye had disappeared by the mid-twentieth century, but in 2012 Ned Wight, a descendant of Frank, relaunched the family legacy in Portland, Maine. Along with rum and gin, he makes Gunpowder rye, an homage to the whiskey his ancestors once made in Baltimore.

New England Distilling Gunpowder Rye

Undisclosed mash bill

AGE		
No age statement		

ALC/VOL

43.5%

NOSE	MOUTHFEEL	FINISH
Putty, acetone, wet cardboard, sour orange, and cereal	Light	Medium, with cocoa and raw grain

GENERAL	PALATE
It needs more age; it's hot and rough-hewn on the palate, even while the nose is fairly restrained. That said, it might show better at a higher proof.	Very big and hot, with cinnamon, nutmeg, minty chocolate

PRICE	RATING
$$	★

New Liberty Distillery

PHILADELPHIA, PENNSYLVANIA

Pennsylvania was once among the top whiskey-producing states, but after Prohibition it fell off the map. New Liberty is part of an in-state renaissance trying to bring back the state's once-ubiquitous rye whiskey style. The names of many of its expressions, including Kinsey and Melvale rye, are taken from actual historic, and now long-defunct, distilleries located in the mid-Atlantic region. All of its grain comes from a farm located about 25 miles from the distillery, just north of Center City Philadelphia.

New Liberty Fortunato's Fate Rye

100 percent rye; finished in sherry casks

AGE	No age statement
ALC/VOL	**47.5**%

NOSE	MOUTHFEEL	FINISH
Dark chocolate, prunes, coffee grounds, a bit of strawberry	Full	Medium; cinnamon

GENERAL	PALATE
Chewy, generous, and it gets better as it sits in the glass.	Dried fruit, dark chocolate, dried cherries, pencil eraser

PRICE	RATING
$$$	

New Liberty Millstone Rye

60 percent malted rye and 40 percent unmalted rye

AGE
No age statement

ALC/VOL
47.5%

NOSE
Oatmeal, cocoa powder, vegetal, cinnamon, mint oil, licorice

MOUTHFEEL
Medium

FINISH
Long; peppery

GENERAL
A solid, if slightly stolid, example of a young, fresh rye—spritely and peppery, even Schweppe-ervescent.

PALATE
Spearmint, pine, grain, wood spice, candied violets

PRICE
$$$

RATING

New Liberty Melvale Straight Rye

51 percent rye and 49 percent corn

AGE
No age statement

ALC/VOL
45%

NOSE
Peanut brittle, wine, butter, cream soda, and a bit of ash that smells better than it sounds

MOUTHFEEL
Medium

FINISH
Lingering, with slight spiciness and bitterness

GENERAL
It has an alluring nose and it's well built, but the palate is uninspired.

PALATE
Not especially sweet, with a thin mouthfeel; there's a light cherry note up front, then cola, yeast, violets and cacao nibs

PRICE
$$$

RATING

New Liberty Kinsey Rye

A blend of three mash bills: 95 percent rye and 5 percent malted barley; 51 percent rye, 45 percent corn, 4 percent malted barley; 51 percent rye and 49 percent malted barley

AGE

4

years old

ALC/VOL

43%

NOSE

Coffee grounds, chocolate, dill, grain silo

MOUTHFEEL

Full

FINISH

Medium; spicy

GENERAL

All three components are sourced from MGP, but they combine to produce something different from the source material: a pleasing whiskey poised between youth and maturity.

PALATE

Dill, mint, unsweetened chocolate, orange bitters

PRICE

$$

RATING

New Riff Distilling

NEWPORT, KENTUCKY

There's a good reason why the New Riff distillery shares a parking lot with the Party Source, one of Kentucky's largest alcohol retailers, located just across the Ohio River from Cincinnati. Its founder, Ken Lewis, owned the Party Source for decades before selling it to his employees to start the distillery. Whether that was a good move for his bank account, it was undoubtedly good for whiskey: New Riff has quickly become a fan favorite, one of the best-regarded distilleries among the new crop of entrants since the whiskey renaissance began in the 2000s.

New Riff Bottled-in-Bond Rye

95 percent rye and 5 percent malted rye

AGE	**4** years old	
ALC/VOL	**50%**	

NOSE	MOUTHFEEL	FINISH
Peanut butter and jelly, roasted nuts, nectarine, toast	Medium-full	Medium; tannic

GENERAL	PALATE	
A solid choice for an after-dinner pour; it tastes like biscotti in a glass, without being too sweet or thick.	Cherry, stewed plum, cinnamon, clove, amaretto	

PRICE	RATING
$$	

New Riff Bottled-in-Bond Malted Rye

100 percent malted rye

AGE
6
years old

ALC/VOL
50%

NOSE
Dried berries, fennel, ketchup, geranium, lemon cake

MOUTHFEEL
Light

FINISH
Medium; lemon pith

GENERAL
Lightly herbal. Fascinating, but it has a thin and astringent quality that is a little fatiguing. Water helps.

PALATE
Honey, floral, lemon-lime, vegetal, vanilla

PRICE
$$$

RATING
★★★

New York Distilling Co.

BROOKLYN, NEW YORK

Like many craft producers, New York Distilling got its start making white spirits—in its case, gin. Unlike at many others, though, the gin at New York Distilling continues to flow: Dorothy Parker and Perry's Tot, its flagships, are among the best craft gins in the country. But the distillery, under co-founder and master distiller Allen Katz, also makes some fantastic rye whiskey, both on its own and pre-mixed in a Rock and Rye, made with candy sugar, cinnamon, and cherries.

New York Distilling Bottled-in-Bond Ragtime Rye

72 percent rye, 16 percent corn, and 12 percent malted barley

AGE		
No age statement		
ALC/VOL		
50%		

NOSE	**MOUTHFEEL**	**FINISH**
Lavender, vanilla, cola, marzipan	Light	Medium; bittersweet chocolate

GENERAL	**PALATE**	
Some interesting flavor notes gracing a fairly young straight-over-home-plate rye. But it fades in the glass.	Mint, pepper, citrus zest, savory	
	PRICE	**RATING**
	$$$	

New York Distilling Ragtime Straight Rye

72 percent rye, 16 percent corn, and 12 percent barley

AGE		
3 years old		

ALC/VOL		
45.2%		

NOSE	MOUTHFEEL	FINISH
Burlap, linseed, black olives, salted cod, apple	Medium	Short; bitter chocolate

GENERAL	PALATE
On first pass, this seems like a well-matured whiskey. But there's not much under the hood; the finish is bitter and the whole thing falls apart with water.	Chocolate and mint, cinnamon, peanuts, blackberry jam

PRICE	RATING
$$	★★

Noble Oak Whiskey

NO LOCATION

Like Cleveland Whiskey and the Green River Spirits Co., Noble Oak uses a proprietary technique to add mature notes its whiskey without the usual time in barrel. The company behind it, Brain Brew Ventures, buys already aged spirit, then applies what it calls the WoodCraft process, which it claims adds "years" to the whiskey. The company also says that it plants a tree for every bottle it sells, which in practice means donating to a tree-planting nonprofit. Noble Oak is owned by the Edrington Group, the Scottish company that owns Macallan and Famous Grouse.

Noble Oak Double Barrel Rye

Undisclosed mash bill

AGE
No age statement

ALC/VOL
48%

NOSE	MOUTHFEEL	FINISH
Melon candy, Lemon Pledge, pine, linen	Light	Short; leather

GENERAL	PALATE	
Spiky and chemical, but it calms down in the glass and shows a more respectable profile. The hops on the palate somehow tie it all together.	Hops, cola, soapy, roasted nuts, cacao	
	PRICE	RATING
		★★

Oak & Eden Finished Whiskey

BRIDGEPORT, TEXAS

Oak & Eden isn't the first company to finish its whiskey with additional exposure to wood. But it's the only one to keep it going after bottling. Each bottle of its sourced whiskey contains a "spire," a spring-shaped curl of wood that the producer claims will continue to add flavor long after the bottle has left the building. The spire allows a long list of possible expressions, pairing various whiskies and wood with different qualities, like species, char level, and finish.

Oak & Eden Rye & Spire

95 percent rye and 5 percent malted barley

AGE	No age statement	
ALC/VOL	**45**%	

NOSE	MOUTHFEEL	FINISH
Apple tobacco, floral, cinnamon candy, wood	Light	Medium; wood char

GENERAL	PALATE	
It's youthful, trying to make up for it with the oak spire. It doesn't succeed.	Herbal tea, tannic, fruit candy, baking spice, orange oil	

PRICE	RATING
$$	

Old Carter Whiskey Co.

NO LOCATION

After co-founding and then selling the phenomenally successful Kentucky Owl brand with their friend Dixon Dedman, Mark and Sherri Carter, two California wine specialists, decided to keep playing the Kentucky whiskey game. Mark handles the logistics, while Sherri runs with marketing and even designs the labels. As they did with Dedman, the Carters buy aging barrels of whiskey, blend them, and sell them under the Old Carter label. They offer both bourbon and rye, and while both are outstanding expressions, it is their rye that truly shines.

Old Carter Straight Rye BATCH 6

Undisclosed mash bill

AGE	
No age statement	

ALC/VOL
58.15%
Varies

NOSE	MOUTHFEEL	FINISH
Dill pickle, grilled chicken, dark chocolate, floral	Medium	Medium; orange

GENERAL	PALATE	
Briny, and with a lot of other surprises—though it is, as a whole, unmistakably a rye. Phenomenal.	Honey, Cel-Ray soda, dill, clove, vanilla saltwater taffy	

PRICE	RATING
$$$$	

Old Elk Distillery

DENVER, COLORADO

Greg Metze, master distiller at Old Elk, is a whiskey veteran, having spent 38 years at MGP Distillery in southern Indiana. When it came time to retire, he decided he wasn't done with making spirits yet, so he headed to Colorado to take up a leadership position at Old Elk. Among other techniques, he instituted a "slow-proofing" process, which adds water to aged whiskey over a period of weeks, not days, a time-consuming step that Metze—and many fans—say creates a mellower, better-integrated flavor profile.

Old Elk Straight Rye

95 percent rye and 5 percent malted barley

AGE	ALC/VOL
No age statement	**50**%

NOSE	MOUTHFEEL	FINISH
Vanilla, perfume, Valencia orange, lemon curd	Medium	Medium; mint

GENERAL	PALATE
Juicy and chewy, it's a delicious whiskey, though it could be more present on the nose.	Mint, milk chocolate, pineapple, cinnamon

PRICE	RATING
$$$	

Old Forester Distillery

LOUISVILLE, KENTUCKY

Old Forester is the oldest continuously produced whiskey brand in America, and the first to be bottled under its own label. It got its start in the 1870s, when a pharmaceutical salesman named George Garvin Brown hit upon the idea of selling whiskey in sealed bottles as a guarantee of quality—at the time, whiskey was sold out of barrels, often with no hint of its origin or authenticity. Brown's operation was the seed for Brown-Forman, today one of the largest spirits companies in America, owning not just Old Forester but Woodford Reserve and Jack Daniel's as well.

Old Forester Straight Rye

65 percent rye, 20 percent malted barley, and 15 percent corn

NOSE	MOUTHFEEL	FINISH
Pencil shavings, pistachio, amaretto, leather	Medium to full	Medium; creamy with a slight burn

GENERAL	PALATE	
An elegant balance of grain and barrel influences, with so many facets to explore. And sold at a great price!	Leather, blackberry jam, pistachio ice cream	

	PRICE	RATING
	$	★★★

AGE
4 years old

ALC/VOL
50%

Old Overholt Whiskey

CLERMONT, KENTUCKY

Old Overholt is one of the great historic whiskeys in American history. First distilled under a different name near Pennsylvania in the early 1800s, it took on its current title in the middle of the century, and could soon be found in bars nationwide. After Prohibition dealt a near-fatal blow to rye whiskey, it came into the hands of National Distillers, a corporate forerunner of Jim Beam, which eventually moved it to Kentucky and changed it to a typical high-corn mash bill.

Old Overholt Bottled-in-Bond Rye

Undisclosed mash bill

AGE		
4 years old		
ALC/VOL		
50%		

NOSE	MOUTHFEEL	FINISH
Grassy, light caramel, lemon verbena, hot cocoa	Medium	Medium; cigar

GENERAL	PALATE
Well balanced, well made, flavorful, and enjoyable—a solid utility player. Drinkable neat, though it would work best in a cocktail.	Cola, gingerbread, white pepper, dark chocolate, tobacco

PRICE	RATING
$	★★★

Old Overholt Straight Rye

Undisclosed mash bill

AGE	**3** years old
ALC/VOL	**43**%

NOSE	MOUTHFEEL	FINISH
Floral, candy shell, honey, dill, mint, soap	Thin-medium	Medium; cloying oak

GENERAL	PALATE
The nose is nice but the palate doesn't match: It's young and brash and off-balance.	Orange peel, wood chips, peanuts, baking chocolate

PRICE	RATING
$	★★

Old Overholt 114 Proof Straight Rye

Undisclosed mash bill

AGE	**3** years old
ALC/VOL	**57**%

NOSE	MOUTHFEEL	FINISH
Rye crackers, molasses, orange Creamsicle, tobacco barn	Medium to full	Long and spicy

GENERAL	PALATE
Juicy, spicy, big, and so very much fun. It needs a splash of water to bring it in balance. But it's a complex, enjoyable rye with so much to give.	Cinnamon, cacao, orange peel, black pepper

PRICE	RATING
$$	★★⯪

Old Pogue Distillery

MAYSVILLE, KENTUCKY

Maysville is a small town on the Ohio River about three hours east of Louisville. It's an old one, too: early in Kentucky's history, its natural port made it an ideal place for settlers to land, and later ship out goods, including whiskey. The original Pogue Distillery dates back to 1876, when Henry Edgar Pogue, a Maysville businessman, bought a local distillery and renamed it. After Prohibition, the distillery sat empty, then burned down in 1973. Some twenty-five years later, Pogue's descendants restarted the brand using sourced stocks. They later bought back the original site, rebuilt the distillery, and began distilling in 2012, producing just a few hundred barrels a year.

Old Maysville Club Bottled-in-Bond Rye Malt

100 percent malted rye

AGE No age statement		
ALC/VOL **50**%		

NOSE	MOUTHFEEL	FINISH
Funky, wet animal skins, leather, cinnamon	Medium	Lingering; orange peel

GENERAL	PALATE	
The nose overwhelms with an almost butyric funk.	Aspirin, vegetal, iron, musty, yeasty bread, sweet mint	

PRICE	RATING
$$$	**NR**

Old Potrero Whiskey

SAN FRANCISCO, CALIFORNIA

Fritz Maytag III and his family are among the great innovators in American food and beverage. His father created Maytag blue cheese on his farm in Iowa; Fritz rescued San Francisco's Anchor Brewing Co. from closure in the 1960s and in 1993 created Anchor Distilling, the home of one of the original whiskeys in the rye revival. The company has since changed hands, and names, but its Old Potrero line remains constant. It also remains old school; Old Potrero uses malted rye, distilled on a copper pot still.

Old Potrero
Single Malt Straight Rye

100 percent malted rye

AGE	ALC/VOL
6 years old	**48.5**%

NOSE	MOUTHFEEL	FINISH
Oatmeal, yeast, red apples, acetone	Medium to full	Short; bitter

GENERAL	PALATE
Unfinished—there's heat but not the backbone or palate complexity to match it.	Baking spices, raw grain, roasted nuts, freshly sawn wood

PRICE	RATING
$$$	★

Old Rip Van Winkle Whiskey

FRANKFORT, KENTUCKY

Julian "Pappy" Van Winkle co-founded the Stitzel-Weller Distillery just after Prohibition, and over the following thirty years built it into a formidable, mid-tier producer of wheated bourbon, then and now considered some of the best available. The distillery was sold after he died, and his son and then grandson, both named Julian, kept the legacy going by buying and bottling whiskey under the Van Winkle name. Today it is among the most sought-after whiskey in America, both its range of bourbons and its rye whiskey, all of which are produced at the Buffalo Trace distillery.

Van Winkle Family Reserve Rye

Undisclosed mash bill

AGE	ALC/VOL
13 years old	**47.8**%

NOSE	MOUTHFEEL	FINISH
Marzipan, cake batter, wood spice, cherry cola	Full	Long; spicy

GENERAL	PALATE
The nose is bourbon-like, sweet and floral, but on the palate the tannins and the lack of any real sweetness make it a rather severe, if still lovely, sip.	Cherry cola, cinnamon, caramel, brightly floral, tannins

PRICE	RATING
$$$$	★★★★

One Eight Distilling

WASHINGTON, DISTRICT OF COLUMBIA

Time was, the Ivy City area in Northeast Washington, D.C., was best known for its animal shelter. Today it is a bustling nook of a neighborhood, with cafes, an axe-throwing gym, and One Eight Distilling. Named for the provision in the Constitution that established the District of Columbia, One Eight makes vodka, gin, and whiskey, as well as a series of limited, one-off releases called Untitled Spirits; recent releases have included a bourbon liqueur and whiskey aged in barrels previously used to hold cacao nibs.

One Eight Distilling District Made Straight Rye

57 percent rye, 29 percent malted rye, and 14 percent corn

AGE	**4** years old
ALC/VOL	**47**%

NOSE	MOUTHFEEL	FINISH
Floral, butterscotch, light tobacco, toasted nuts, vanilla batter	Light	Long; mint

GENERAL	PALATE
Down the middle, pleasant, but not remarkable. It would make a fine mixer.	Mexican chocolate, black pepper, cinnamon gum, mint

PRICE	RATING
$$	★★

Oppidan Spirits

WAUKEGAN, ILLINOIS

Illinois was once the largest whiskey state in the country, thanks to the enormous distilleries located in and around Peoria. While few want to go back to those days—Peoria whiskey was often a step up from rotgut—there is a growing number of craft distilleries bringing the Land of Lincoln back to the whiskey game. Oppidan, located northwest of Chicago, is one of them. Founded in 2015, it takes an innovative approach to distilling and maturation, using techniques like solera aging and offbeat finishing barrels to create a line of unique spirits.

Oppidan Malted Rye

100 percent malted rye

AGE		
No age statement		
ALC/VOL		
47%		

NOSE	MOUTHFEEL	FINISH
Banana, charred oak, grain silo, vanilla, citrus compote	Medium	Short; some heat

GENERAL	PALATE	
A solid example of the next generation of American craft rye. Grain- and fruit-forward, with a coherent evolution from nose to finish.	Fresh bread, Juicy Fruit, chocolate, dried chile	
	PRICE	RATING
	$$	★★★

Kentucky Peerless Distilling Co.

LOUISVILLE, KENTUCKY

The modern incarnation of Kentucky Peerless is the brainchild of Corky Taylor, a Louisville businessman who yearned to resurrect his family's whiskey brand. The original Peerless was among the largest in the state, but it shut down just before Prohibition. Taylor, the great-grandson of the original owner, relaunched the company in the 2010s, with distilling starting in 2015 under the guidance of master distiller Caleb Kilburn. The first two rye releases won widespread praise, although Taylor conceded that it is Peerless's bourbon that pays the bills. "This is bourbon country," he said.

Kentucky Peerless Barrel Proof Straight Rye

BARREL R150813103

Undisclosed mash bill

AGE
No age statement

ALC/VOL
54.1%
Varies

NOSE	MOUTHFEEL	FINISH
Cinnamon, vanilla, cola, amaretto	Full	Medium; dark chocolate

GENERAL	PALATE
Big, bold, and friendly, though at this level of alcohol it should be showing more structure and depth.	Pencil shavings, melon, hazelnut, vanilla bean

PRICE
$$$$

RATING

Pikesville Rye Whiskey

BARDSTOWN, KENTUCKY

Pikesville was once a popular whiskey distilled in Baltimore, using a Maryland style. Unlike most Maryland ryes, it survived Prohibition, but just barely. It limped through the rest of the century, with strong sales in the Baltimore area despite its acquisition by Heaven Hill, its shift in production to Kentucky, and its mash bill change to a high-corn rye. For several years, it could only be found in and around the city, though after a relaunch and a bump up in proof, Heaven Hill is selling it more widely.

Pikesville Straight Rye

51 percent rye, 37 percent corn, and 12 percent malted barley

AGE
No age statement

ALC/VOL
55%

NOSE
Pancake batter, vanilla, blackberry jam, peanuts

MOUTHFEEL
Light

FINISH
Long; spicy and slightly tannic

GENERAL
A classic Kentucky rye, with strong bourbon overtones.

PALATE
Cinnamon, root beer, Juicy Fruit, grilled pineapple

PRICE
$$

RATING
★★★

Pinhook

NO LOCATION

Sean Josephs, the founder of Pinhook, got his start in wine.
He spent a decade as a sommelier before opening Char
No. 4, a whiskey bar and restaurant in Brooklyn, New York,
in 2008. He eventually decided to bring his wine expertise
to whiskey by creating Pinhook. Pinhooking is the process
of identifying and fostering gifted racehorses, and Josephs
takes the same approach to whiskey. Instead of distilling,
he chooses promising young barrels of whiskey, which he
blends and releases in annual vintages. At first he bought
from MGP, but in 2016 he switched to Castle & Key, which
occupies the former Old Taylor distillery outside Frankfort,
Kentucky.

Pinhook
Straight Rye Whiskey
Vertical Series

Undisclosed mash bill

AGE	ALC/VOL
4 years old	**48.5**% *Varies*

NOSE	MOUTHFEEL	FINISH
Floral perfume, Sauternes, cedar, lavender, linen	Light	Long; ginger

GENERAL	PALATE
Elegant and effervescent, light but never superficial. A wonderful expression of rye's delicate side.	Orange blossom, ginger, coffee grounds, rock sugar, pistachio

PRICE	RATING
$$	

Putnam New England Whiskey

BOSTON, MASSACHUSETTS

In 2012 Boston Beer Co. veteran Rhonda Kallman founded Boston Harbor Distillery, which produces Putnam whiskey, making her one of the first women to enter the craft distilling scene. The distillery is located in an old mill building on the waterfront in Dorchester, a once-run-down neighborhood that is now rapidly gentrifying. Its whiskeys, including single malts and ryes, are named for Silas Putnam, a nineteenth-century Boston inventor.

Putnam New England Straight Rye

95 percent rye and 5 percent malted barley

AGE	No age statement
ALC/VOL	**43**%

NOSE	MOUTHFEEL	FINISH
Burlap, talcum, aspirin, hay, lavender	Medium	Short; citrus

GENERAL		
It shows some intriguing freshness on the nose, but the palate is one-dimensional, hinting at depth without going there.	Chocolate powder, Jordan almond, soap, malt	
	PRICE	RATING
	$$	★★

Rabbit Hole Distillery

LOUISVILLE, KENTUCKY

Kaveh Zamanian was born in Iran and raised in Los Angeles, trained as a psychologist, and worked in Chicago. Scotch was always his drink, he said, until his wife, Heather, introduced him to bourbon—and pulled him down a "rabbit hole" that ended with him leaving his job in Chicago and moving to Louisville in 2008. He founded Rabbit Hole in 2012, buying sourced spirits while he went about building the distillery. In just a few years, Zamanian made himself a fixture in the Kentucky distilling scene, and Rabbit Hole, is one of the leading names in the state's new generation of craft distilleries. Though he eventually sold it to spirits conglomerate Pernod Ricard, he retains creative control.

Rabbit Hole Boxergrail Straight Rye

95 percent rye and 5 percent malted barley

AGE	
3 years old	

ALC/VOL	
47.5% *Varies*	

NOSE	MOUTHFEEL	FINISH
Perfume, pineapple, talcum powder, lilac	Medium to full	Long and spicy, with fruit juice

GENERAL	PALATE
Delightfully floral, possibly too much so, but it is still an enjoyable, effervescent dram.	Pineapple, cream soda, ginger, mint

PRICE	RATING
$$	

Ranger Creek Brewing & Distilling

SAN ANTONIO, TEXAS

It says something about the newness of the Texas distilling scene that Ranger Creek, founded in 2010, is among the oldest distilleries in the state. The distillery, located in north San Antonio, is just one half of the operation; there's a brewery too, making it what some people call a "brewstillery." They sure do love guns: The whiskeys bear names like ".36 Bourbon" and "Rimfire Single Malt" and come with "small caliber" and "large caliber" labels, denoting the size of the barrels they were aged in.

Ranger Creek .44 Rye

100 percent rye

AGE	No age statement
ALC/VOL	**47**%

NOSE	MOUNTHFEEL	FINISH
Cherry, grilled vegetables, apple cider, pencil shavings	Light	Brief; tannic

GENERAL	PALATE	
Its immaturity does it a disservice, because beneath the barrel there is evidence of real potential.	Cinnamon, cocoa powder, new wood, espresso	
	PRICE **$$**	RATING ★⭑

Ransom Wine Co. & Distillery

MCMINNVILLE, OREGON

Ransom didn't start out making whiskey—or vodka. It began by distilling local fruit into grappa, eau de vie, and brandy. Founded in 1997, it didn't take up grain until a decade later; along the way its owner, Tad Seestedt, made a pitstop in wine. True to its roots in European distilling traditions, Ransom makes all its spirits, including whiskey, in a French alembic still, typically used for Cognac and eau de vie.

Ransom Henry DuYore's Rye

A blend of MGP rye and the distillery's own whiskey, made wih a mash bill of 78 percent rye and 22 percent malted barley

AGE	**2** years old
ALC/VOL	**46.1**%

NOSE	MOUTHFEEL	FINISH
Apple juice, varnish, wet grain, varnish, plastic, cheap perfume	Medium	Medium; cloying

GENERAL	PALATE
Loud and disorganized, this is a challenging whiskey to make sense of, and not especially worth the effort.	Plastic, burnt grain, Hawaiian Punch, celery root

PRICE	RATING
$$	**NR**

Rebel Whiskey

BARDSTOWN, KENTUCKY

For decades, Rebel—formerly known as Rebel Yell—was marketed to Southern white drinkers, with its unmistakably Lost Cause image winning adherents long after it became unacceptable to espouse neo-Confederate sentiments in public. In an attempt to move away from that image, Luxco, which produces the whiskey at its Lux Row distillery, dropped the "Yell" from the brand name and emphasized the "Rebel" part of the name. Whether that's better or not, the whiskey remains a strong seller.

Rebel Straight Rye

95 percent rye and 5 percent malted barley

AGE	**2** years old
ALC/VOL	**45**%

NOSE	MOUTHFEEL	FINISH
Roses, fruit candy, caramel, roasted herbs, toasted oak	Light	Short; cola

GENERAL	PALATE	
The nose is shy and the palate is on the thin side, but otherwise this is a well-done, classic rye.	Cinnamon stick, Juicy Fruit, treacle, pencil shavings	

PRICE	RATING
$	★★

Redemption Whiskey

NO LOCATION

Sometimes building a successful brand is all about luck and timing—having the right stuff at the right time. That's what Dave Schmier and Michael Kanbar did when they created Redemption, one of the first modern whiskey brands to embrace rye. Their company, Bardstown Bourbon Selections, started buying the spirit from MGP, back when it was called Lawrenceburg Distillers Indiana and no one gave much thought to rye. As interest in the category grew, they added more, older expressions. Eventually they sold the company to Deutsch Family Wine & Spirits, which owns Masterson's (page 150), and Schmier went on to found Proof and Wood Ventures (pages 200 and 206).

Redemption
10-Year-Old
Barrel Proof Rye BATCH 002

95 percent rye and 5 percent malted barley

AGE
10
years old

ALC/VOL
58.1%

NOSE
Butterscotch, sweet wood char, cinnamon, raspberry

MOUTHFEEL
Light to medium

FINISH
Medium; slightly dry

GENERAL
The nose is shy and the palate is on the thin side, but otherwise this is a well-done, classic rye.

PALATE
Butterscotch, marzipan, raspberry, Red Hots

PRICE
$$$

RATING

Redemption Straight Rye

BATCH NO. 260

95 percent rye and 5 percent malted barley

AGE	
No age statement	

ALC/VOL
46%

NOSE	MOUTHFEEL	FINISH
Chocolate, dried orange peel, potpourri, burlap, putty	Medium	Medium; allspice

GENERAL	PALATE
Classic nose, classic palate, but it doesn't stand out from the pack. Still, a solid, mild pour, good for beginners asking what this rye thing is all about.	Orange pekoe tea, allspice, cocoa powder, wood spices

PRICE	RATING
$	

Redemption Rye Rum Cask Finish

95 percent rye and 5 percent malted barley; finished in rum casks

AGE	
No age statement	

ALC/VOL
47%

NOSE	MOUTHFEEL	FINISH
Jam, Sauternes, dill, celery, sweet tea	Light	Medium; sweet

GENERAL	PALATE
Young and fruity, sweet and creamy, but overall it's one-dimensional.	Grain, dill, grapefruit, peach

PRICE	RATING
$$	

Red River Whiskey

One of many sourced brands coming out of Texas these days, Red River is bottled in Dallas but distilled at an undisclosed location. The brand is owned by Shaw-Ross, a wine and spirits importer based in Florida.

Red River Texas Rye

95 percent rye and 5 percent malted barley

AGE	No age statement
ALC/VOL	**40**%

NOSE	MOUTHFEEL	FINISH
Rum, dill, fennel, mint, cocoa powder, pineapple	Light	Short; bitter

GENERAL	PALATE
Astringent and vegetal, with a fringe of bright sweetness. It's competent and pleasing but ultimately lacking oomph.	Grain, stewed vegetable, lemon oil, honeydew, orange rind

PRICE	RATING
$$	★★

Redwood Empire Whiskey

GRATON, CALIFORNIA

Located in western Sonoma County, not far from the towering trees that give the whiskey its name, Graton Distilling Co., which makes Redwood Empire, stands out as a world-class distillery in a sea of world-class wineries. Each of its expressions is named after an iconic redwood tree—Emerald Giant, Pipe Dream, Lost Monarch—and the distillery says that a portion of its profit goes to planting trees. Its whiskeys are mostly blends of sourced and estate-made spirits.

Redwood Empire Emerald Giant Rye

95 percent rye and 5 percent malted barley

AGE		
No age statement		
ALC/VOL		
45%		

NOSE	MOUTHFEEL	FINISH
Linseed, cinnamon, cedar, dry orange peel	Full	Short; unsweetened chocolate

GENERAL	PALATE
A competent, conventional young rye with a light, zesty profile.	Cinnamon, black pepper, orange bitters, spearmint

PRICE	RATING
$$	★★★

Reservoir Distillery

RICHMOND, VIRGINIA

Over the last decade, Richmond, Virginia, has transformed from a sleepy Southern city into a booming culinary destination, with dozens of breweries and distilleries—Reservoir among them. The distillery launched in 2008 and is decidedly old school, using traditional methods like slow, open-top fermentation and a copper pot still. Its mash bills are all single grain: The wheat uses only wheat, and the rye only rye.

Reservoir Rye

100 percent rye

AGE	No age statement
ALC/VOL	**50**%

NOSE	MOUTHFEEL	FINISH
Butterscotch, vanilla, raisins, tobacco, brown sugar	Full	Long; cola

GENERAL	PALATE
This whiskey does everything you ask of it and more: vivacious yet mature, chewy but balanced, tannic without sucking at your teeth.	Sherry, fruit cake, orange zest, mint, ginger, cinnamon

PRICE	RATING
$$	★★★

Rittenhouse

BARDSTOWN, KENTUCKY

Like Old Overholt, Rittenhouse is a former Pennsylvania rye whiskey that fell into out-of-state hands after Prohibition and eventually migrated westward, and toward a higher corn content in its mashbill. Today it is owned and distilled by Heaven Hill. It remains a bartender and drinker favorite, in part because of its high proof, making it an excellent component in strongly flavored cocktails.

Rittenhouse Bottled-in-Bond Rye

Undisclosed mash bill

AGE	ALC/VOL
4 years old	**50**%

NOSE	MOUTHFEEL	FINISH
Red apple, cherry juice, graham crackers, black tea	Light to medium	Medium; tannic

GENERAL	PALATE
Big and bright, but still chewy; a bit superficial but still tasty. There's more complexity here than first appears.	Cinnamon, black pepper, orange bitters, spearmint

PRICE	RATING
$$	

Riverset

MEMPHIS, TENNESSEE

Memphis is not known as a whiskey-making town, though it does a fair amount of whiskey drinking. In fact, the producer of Riverset Rye, B.R. Distilling, founded in 2014, is the oldest distillery in the city. The company makes a bourbon and a rye of its own, and it contract-distills for a number of private-label brands as well.

Riverset Straight Rye

95 percent rye and 5 percent malted barley

AGE	No age statement
ALC/VOL	**46.5**%

NOSE	MOUTHFEEL	FINISH
Toasted herbs, coconut, banana, lime zest, brown sugar	Light	Short; coconut

GENERAL	PALATE
It's whisper-light on the nose and surprisingly sweet and full on the palate. But the flavors don't line up.	Fruit cocktail syrup, duck sauce, apricot, cashew

PRICE	RATING
$$	★★

Rock Town Distillery

LITTLE ROCK, ARKANSAS

Little Rock is known as Rock Town, and so is its oldest and largest distillery. Arkansas isn't exactly a whiskey state, but Rock Town has been churning out the stuff to great acclaim for over a decade. Founded in 2010 by Phil Brandon, it gets all its grain from within 125 miles of the distillery to make its bourbon, rye, vodka, and liqueurs.

Rock Town
Single Barrel Rye BARREL 133

52 percent rye, 38 percent corn, and 10 percent
malted barley

AGE	
16 months	

ALC/VOL	
62.3%	
Varies	

NOSE	MOUTHFEEL	FINISH
Prunes, linen, pipe tobacco, marzipan, maple syrup	Full	Long, with fruitcake and mint

GENERAL	PALATE
Rich, loaded with Christmas spices and fruit, but it's missing a depth that would move it into the top ranks.	Butterscotch, tobacco, stewed fruits, Concord grapes

PRICE	RATING
$$$	

Rock Town
Arkansas Straight Rye

52 percent rye, 38 percent corn, and 10 percent
malted barley

AGE	
No age statement	

ALC/VOL	
46%	

NOSE	MOUTHFEEL	FINISH
Popsicle sticks, sunflower seeds, nutty, and grassy	Light to medium	Lingers, with cinnamon warmth

GENERAL	PALATE
This whiskey is too young, showing a grainy funk that is sometimes masked by too much wood.	Grain and wood tannins up front, with some mid-palate sweetness

PRICE	RATING
$	

Rogue Spirits

NEWPORT, OREGON

Rogue is best known for its beer, especially its iconic Dead Guy ale. But the brewery has also been making spirits since 2003, many of them derived from a beer base. For starters, there's a Dead Guy whiskey, essentially a distilled and aged version of the original Dead Guy. Its Rolling Thunder Stouted whiskey is aged in barrels that once held a hefty imperial stout.

Rogue Spirits Oregon Rye Malt

52 percent malted rye and 48 percent malted barley

AGE
No age statement

ALC/VOL
40%

NOSE
Lemon, eucalyptus, white pepper, almond

MOUTHFEEL
Light

FINISH
Medium; lemon oil

GENERAL
It tastes almost like a distilled beer, certainly more than it does a rye. It's young and unconventional.

PALATE
Hops, Necco wafers, grapefruit, malt

PRICE
$$

RATING
★★⯪

Rossville Union

LAWRENCEBURG, INDIANA

Midwest Grain Products, based in Kansas, is the corporate owner of this massive distillery in southern Indiana that was once owned by Seagram. Until recently, MGP's rye whiskey was everywhere, and nowhere—all of its production was sold to private clients, who aged and/or bottled it under their own labels. Even today, many of the whiskey brands in this book are or were once made by MGP. Eventually, MGP decided to get into the game itself with its Rossville Union line of rye, and in 2020 it purchased Lux Row, the maker of Ezra Brooks, Daviess County, and other whiskey brands. In 2021, MGP renamed its distillery Ross & Squibb, a nod to its historic roots.

Rossville Union Barrel Proof Rye

A blend of MGP's two rye mash bills, one at 51 percent rye, 45 percent corn, and 5 percent malted barley, the other at 95 percent rye and 5 percent malted barley

AGE	ALC/VOL
5 years old	**56.3**%

NOSE	MOUTHFEEL	FINISH
Old leather, cold fireplace, mint, Concord grapes	Full	Medium; mint

GENERAL	PALATE
It offers an attractive set of flavors, presented with complexity yet clarity.	Honey, cola, horehound, After Eight mints

PRICE	RATING
$$$	★★⯪

Rossville Union Straight Rye

A blend of MGP's two rye mash bills, one at 51 percent rye, 45 percent corn, and 5 percent malted barley, the other at 95 percent rye and 5 percent malted barley

AGE	ALC/VOL
No age statement	**47**%

NOSE	MOUTHFEEL	FINISH
Rich cocoa, honey peanuts, winey, pine, light tobacco	Light	Medium; cinnamon apple

GENERAL	PALATE
Thin and over-oaked. What's there is tasty, but it's indistinct. It would be fine as an absent-minded nightcap.	Oranges, cherry, cinnamon, cider, coconut

PRICE	RATING
$$	★★

Rough Rider

BAITING HOLLOW, NEW YORK

It's either a blessing or a curse for a distillery to live smack in the middle of a major wine region, but Long Island Spirits, the maker of Rough Rider whiskey, has been making it work since 2007. Founded by Richard Stabile on the western edge of the island's North Fork, the distillery benefits from being the odd duck amid an endless line of vineyards—the place to stop when you can't stand to taste another merlot. Stabile started his company with vodka before turning to brown liquor, most of which he bottles under the Rough Rider label with names like Bull Moose and Big Stick, references to another of the island's legacies, Theodore Roosevelt, who lived in (relatively) nearby Oyster Bay.

Rough Rider Bull Moose Three Barrel Rye

93 percent rye and 7 percent malted barley; aged sequentially in new oak, ex-bourbon, and ex-single malt barrels

AGE	ALC/VOL
No age statement	**45**%

NOSE	MOUTHFEEL	FINISH
Lavender, Lemon Pledge, mint, pipe tobacco	Full	Medium; bitter

GENERAL	PALATE
It smells like craft whiskey, but with good wood integration; the palate offers some interesting notes but it's flabby and muddled.	Mexican chocolate, celery, cream, bran muffin

PRICE	RATING
$$	

Rough Rider
The Big Stick Rye

93 percent rye and 7 percent malted barley;
fermented with Champagne yeast

AGE	ALC/VOL
No age statement	**60.5**%

NOSE	MOUTHFEEL	FINISH
Rubber, eucalyptus, ash, candied citrus peel	Medium-full	Medium; wood char

GENERAL	PALATE
The nose starts sweet but darkens and dries in the glass. The palate is more interesting than delicious.	Grain, grass, mint, fennel, rubber

PRICE	RATING
$$$	★★

Roulette Whiskey

NO LOCATION

Dave Schmier was among the first people to realize the possibility of buying and bottling whiskey from what was then called Lawrenceburg Distillers Indiana, and is today called Ross & Squibb or, more broadly, MGP, after its corporate owners. His first line, Redemption, was a massive hit. After selling it, he moved on to create even more brands through his company Proof and Wood Ventures. As he did with the Deadwood line of whiskeys (page 98), Schmier created Roulette as a reasonably priced, versatile rye whiskey—tasty enough to drink on its own, robust enough to sit comfortably in a cocktail.

Roulette Straight Rye

95 percent rye and 5 percent malted barley

AGE
No age statement

ALC/VOL
50%

NOSE	MOUTHFEEL	FINISH
Molasses, dried hay, turpentine, pumpernickel, mint	Medium to full	Long; orange rind

GENERAL	PALATE	
Tastes like Christmas, without the overt fruitcake notes. Bready, yeasty, tasty.	Anise, dill, port, candied orange, tobacco	
	PRICE	RATING
	$	

Ry3

NO LOCATION

Karthik Sudhir, an Indian immigrant, founded Phenomenal
Spirits in 2018, debuting with a 10-year-old rum called Ron
Izalco. To perfect his Ry3 whiskey, a multi-component blend, he
hired Matt Witzig, formerly of Jos. A. Magnus & Co. The whiskey
in the rye is a blend of spirits from Alberta Distillers and MGP,
and a light whiskey, all finished in a rum cask—making it not a
true rye, but a blended whiskey. "We're not going to compete,
we're going to create our own niche," Sudhir said in a 2021
interview with the Birdies & Bourbon podcast.

Phenomenal Spirits Ry3

Blend of undisclosed mash bills; finished in a rum cask

AGE		No age statement
ALC/VOL		**50**%

NOSE	MOUTHFEEL	FINISH
Demarara sugar, banana, acetone, rubbery phenolsl	Light	Medium; bitter grains

GENERAL	PALATE
Relatively young, but some attractive and weird flavors—rum, who'd have thunk it?	Rum rubberiness, candy shell, dill, cereal grains, citrus, juicy fruit

PRICE	RATING
$$$	

Sagamore Spirit Distillery

BALTIMORE, MARYLAND

Baltimore was once hopping with distilleries, almost all of them making rye. In fact, Maryland rye was among the best-recognized whiskey styles in America. But that ended with Prohibition. Today a few distilleries are pushing to resurrect that tradition, including Sagamore. Located on the Baltimore waterfront not far from downtown, it makes a wide variety of whiskeys, but almost all of them are some form of rye whiskey.

Sagamore Spirit Rye

A blend of three mash bills: 95 percent rye and 5 percent malted barley; 51 percent rye, 45 percent corn, and 4 percent malted barley; and 51 percent rye and 49 percent malted barley

AGE	
4 years old	

ALC/VOL	
41.5%	

NOSE	MOUTHFEEL	FINISH
Solvent, dill, cedar, licorice, orange blossom	Light	Medium; nutmeg

GENERAL	PALATE
It's not unenjoyable, but it's flabby, one-dimensional, and rather dull.	Dried orange peel, almond, grassy, minty heat

PRICE	RATING
$$	

Sagamore Spirit Cask Strength Rye

AGE	**4** years old

A blend of three mash bills: 95 percent rye and 5 percent malted barley; 51 percent rye, 45 percent corn, and 4 percent malted barley; and 51 percent rye and 49 percent malted barley

ALC/VOL	**56.1**%

NOSE	MOUTHFEEL	FINISH
Acetone, linseed oil, lemon, rhubarb	Light	Long and sweet

GENERAL	PALATE
The nose and finish are shy—and yet it somehow still works. Tasty and fun.	Vanilla, Cel-Ray soda, mint, lemon, menthol

PRICE	RATING
$$$	

Sagamore Spirit Cognac Finish Rye

AGE	No age statement

A blend of three mash bills: 95 percent rye and 5 percent malted barley; 51 percent rye, 45 percent corn, and 4 percent malted barley; and 51 percent rye and 49 percent malted barley. Finished in ex-Cognac barrels

ALC/VOL	**50.5**%

NOSE	MOUTHFEEL	FINISH
Butterscotch, grape, acetone, lavender, iron	Light	Medium; apples

GENERAL	PALATE
Unbalanced, but there are some interesting flavors and evolution with water and time in the glass. There is a pleasant, restrained bitterness toward the end.	Tannic, juicy, brown sugar, Big Red, vanilla

PRICE	RATING
$$$	

Sagamore Spirit Double Oak Rye

A blend of three mash bills: 95 percent rye and 5 percent malted barley; 51 percent rye, 45 percent corn, and 4 percent malted barley; and 51 percent rye and 49 percent malted barley. Aged 4-5 years, then re-casked in a "wave-stave" barrel.

AGE
4-5 years old

ALC/VOL
48.3%

NOSE
Brown sugar, perfume, leather, slightly earthy

MOUTHFEEL
Medium

FINISH
Long and peppery

GENERAL
A compelling whiskey with a unique smoky nose. Some people might find it too woody.

PALATE
Root beer, smoked almonds, baking spices, grainy

PRICE
$$$

RATING

Sagamore Spirit Bottled-in-Bond Rye

A blend of three mash bills: 95 percent rye and 5 percent malted barley; 51 percent rye, 45 percent corn, and 4 percent malted barley; and 51 percent rye and 49 percent malted barley

AGE
No age statement

ALC/VOL
50%

NOSE
Green banana, custard, lavender, honeysuckle

MOUTHFEEL
Medium

FINISH
Long; sweet mint

GENERAL
Yummy! It tastes like chocolate mint candies, but it's not too sweet. The herbal, minty quality gives it a strong, alluring backbone.

PALATE
Butterscotch, mint, fennel, chocolate

PRICE
$$$

RATING

Savage & Cooke Distillery

VALLEJO, CALIFORNIA

Dave Phinney is a wine guy, considered one of the best California wine makers of his generation. But after several years working the grape trade, he decided to branch out to spirits. In 2018 he founded Savage & Cooke on Mare Island, in the northeast corner of San Francisco Bay. As he does with wines, he aims for his whiskey to be full of lush, rounded aromas and intense flavors, often created by finishing in wine barrels.

Savage & Cooke Lip Service Rye

51 percent rye, 45 percent corn, and 4 percent malted barley

AGE		
3 years old		
ALC/VOL		
45%		

NOSE	MOUTHFEEL	FINISH
Pine, sandalwood, cedar, dried peanut shells	Light	Short; bitter

GENERAL	PALATE	
Serviceable but unremarkable, though it shows promise if it's allowed to age longer.	Violet candy, honey, bitter tobacco, orange peel	

PRICE	RATING
$$	★★

The Senator Whiskey

NO LOCATION

The Senator Rye is the partner expression to the Ambassador, a 12-year-old bourbon. Both are made by Proof and Wood, the company run by Dave Schmier, who previously founded the Redemption line of whiskey. Both are unofficial follow-ups to the Presidential Dram, a whiskey released to commemorate the 2016 presidential election.

The Senator

95 percent rye and 5 percent malted barley

AGE	**6** years old
ALC/VOL	**60.7**%

NOSE	MOUTHFEEL	FINISH
Orange tea, dried cherries, sweet tobacco, cinnamon	Light	Medium, spicy

GENERAL	PALATE	
Bold, spicy and not at all calming down despite its age. Yet even at such a high proof, it doesn't require water. There's a lot going on and it pays to experience it full throttle.	Clove, mint chocolate, sawdust, dried orange slices	
	PRICE	RATING
	$$$	★★★

Smooth Ambler Spirits

MAXWELTON, WEST VIRGINIA

Smooth Ambler is both a distillery and a non-distilling producer—or, as it likes to call itself, a merchant bottler, buying barrels from other distilleries and aging them further. Much of that whiskey, both bourbon and rye, appears under the distillery's Old Scout label. These days Smooth Ambler makes a good amount of its own whiskey at its facility in Maxwelton, not far from the Greenbrier, a historic mountain resort. In 2017 Pernod Ricard, the French spirits giant, bought a controlling share of Smooth Ambler.

Smooth Ambler Contradiction Rye

A blend of four rye mash bills

AGE	ALC/VOL
No age statement	**52.5**%

NOSE	MOUTHFEEL	FINISH
Tomato, dill, linen, candy corn, celery	Light	Medium; saltwater taffy

GENERAL	PALATE
It has a shy, delicate nose, on the savory side, but the palate evolves toward fruit sweetness—a compelling whiskey	Lemon, cherry candy, tangerine, quince paste

PRICE	RATING
$$	

Smooth Ambler Old Scout Single Barrel Cask Strength Straight Rye

95 percent rye and 5 percent malted barley

AGE	ALC/VOL
5 years old *Varies*	**57.7**% *Varies*

NOSE	MOUTHFEEL	FINISH
Wood spices, tomato vine, shellac, marigold	Full	Long; dill

GENERAL	PALATE
A beast, but manageable; it definitely needs water. It's on the dry side and lacks the depth needed for a great cask strength whiskey.	Apricot, dill, almond, fresh-cut wood

PRICE	RATING
$$$	

Sono 1420 American Craft Distillers

NORWALK, CONNECTICUT

Every startup distillery needs and angle, and for Sono 1420, that angle is hemp. Each bottle contains actual, full hemp seeds, enough so that the federal government doesn't let them call the result whiskey—it has to be called a "hemped rye spirit," distilled from rye, corn, and hemp seed, and finished in oak barrels. The result won't get you high, but if nothing else it gives a certain élan that may make the rest of the whiskey in your flight taste delicious.

Sono 1420 Hemped Rye Spirit

75 percent rye, 15 percent corn, and 10 percent hemp seed

AGE	No age statement
ALC/VOL	**46%**

NOSE	MOUTHFEEL	FINISH
White pepper, paper, acetone, grass	Light	Short; orange pith

GENERAL	PALATE	
It's pleasingly superficial, but it breaks down with water and offers too short and bitter a finish.	Lemon, honey, mint, coconut	

PRICE	RATING
$$	★☆

Sonoma Distilling Co.

ROHNERT PARK, CALIFORNIA

Sonoma Distilling leans hard on its location, smack in the middle of California wine country. It was among the first of a wave of new distilleries in the state and the first to take root in Sonoma County. Critical to that success was founder and distiller Adam Spiegel, a Bay Area native who, in times past, might have gone into winemaking, but these days finds whiskey a more attractive, wide-open opportunity. In addition to rye, the distillery makes a bourbon and a wheat whiskey, as well as a few wood-smoked versions and an annual, limited-release series.

Sonoma Rye

80 percent rye and 20 percent malted rye

AGE	No age statement
ALC/VOL	**48**%

NOSE	MOUTHFEEL	FINISH
Vegetal, fennel seed, toasted grain, grape candy, sawdust	Light	Medium; very sweet

GENERAL	PALATE
It smells and tastes very young, with a butyric, vegetal nose that only partly dissipates and ruins the rest of the experience.	Stewed orange, turpentine, pencil shavings, ethanol heat

PRICE	RATING
$$	**NR**

Spirit Works Distillery

SEBASTOPOL, CALIFORNIA

Located just north of Sonoma Distilling Co., Spirit Works is another early entrant to the Northern California distilling boom. Founded in 2012, it is a labor of love for Timo and Ashby Marshall, the husband-and-wife team who still get down and dirty with the mash, fermentation, and still, as well as getting friendly with visitors and fans. Spirit Works has developed a strong local following, and in 2020 it was named "Distillery of the Year" by the American Distilling Institute.

Spirit Works Straight Rye

70 percent rye and 30 percent malted barley

AGE	**4** years old	
ALC/VOL	**45**%	

NOSE	MOUTHFEEL	FINISH
Vanilla, baking bread, fennel, mushrooms, grassy	Light	Dry and peppery

GENERAL	PALATE
Pleasant, balanced, and quaffable; a good summer rye.	Unsweetened chocolate, pecans, pipe tobacco, celery seeds

PRICE	RATING
$$$	★★★

Starlight Distillery

BORDEN, INDIANA

Starlight Distillery is just one part of an alcoholic empire located in rural southern Indiana. Alongside an orchard, vineyard, and winery, the distillery draws on traditions going back generations in the Huber family, who settled the area in the 1830s and have long produced wine, cider, whiskey, and other spirits for local customers. That's changing: Starlight's whiskeys have begun to rack up awards and critical recognition, as well as demand, and it may not be long before its whiskey appears on a liquor store shelf near you.

Starlight Old Rickhouse Straight Rye

Undisclosed mash bill

AGE	No age statement
ALC/VOL	**46**%

NOSE	MOUTHFEEL	FINISH
Honeycomb, roasted nuts, mint, leather, chocolate-covered cherries	Full	Short; nutty

GENERAL	PALATE
Silky but spicy, engaging but complex. It drinks heavy, but with a classic rye profile that rewards repeat visits.	Red Hots, cola, chocolate-covered nuts, smoke, dill, caramel

PRICE	RATING
$$	★★★★

Stellum

LOUISVILLE, KENTUCKY

Some whiskey companies make their own whiskey; some buy it from other distilleries and only bottle it themselves. Barrell Craft Spirits, producer of Stellum, has led the way in a third direction. Working with several dozen distilleries around the country, the Louisville-based company buys whiskey to blend into a wide variety of limited and regular-release expressions. Blending may have once been a bad word in America, but Barrell's model comes from Scotland, where blending is considered an art. Barrell (that's right, with two L's, a spelling that its founder, Joe Beatrice, finds distinctive) bottled its first case in 2014, and has grown quickly into one of the most renowned brands in American whiskey. The Stellum brand, launched in 2021, is intended to be a more consistent offering, at a lower price, than Barrell's line of one-off whiskey blends.

Stellum Rye

A blend of whiskeys from Indiana, Kentucky, and Tennessee

AGE
No age statement

ALC/VOL
58.1%

NOSE	MOUTHFEEL	FINISH
Dill, hemp, rye, celery seed, roses, potpourri, tea	Medium	Medium; cinnamon

GENERAL	PALATE	
Explosively sweet on the entry, evolving into a rich and yummy serenade with an herbal backbone.	Red Hots, pastry, black tea, pineapple, vanilla	

PRICE
$$$

RATING

Stoll & Wolfe Distillery

LITITZ, PENNSYLVANIA

Dick Stoll was one of the greatest distillers in American history, and among the last living links to Pennsylvania's heyday as a whiskey powerhouse. He spent most of his career at the the original Michter's distillery, working there until it closed in 1990. He worked in other industries, then retired, figuring his distilling days were long over. Then, in 2013, Erik Wolfe, an aspiring whiskey maker, contacted him with an irresistible offer: help restart Pennsylvania rye by distilling their own whiskey, from scratch. Stoll passed away in 2020, just as Stoll & Wolfe was preparing to release their new whiskey.

Stoll & Wolfe Pennsylvania Rye

60 percent rye, 25 percent corn, and 10 percent malted barley

AGE		
8 months old		
ALC/VOL		
45%		

NOSE	MOUTHFEEL	FINISH
Ruby red grapefruit, orange oil, talcum powder, soft pretzel	Light to medium	Medium; pepper-mint

GENERAL	PALATE	
Intriguing and unconventional, a semi-dry rye with subtle fruit and citrus layers.	Pine, cocoa powder, cinnamon, cherry candy, perfume	

PRICE	RATING
$$$	

Taconic Distillery

STANFORDVILLE, NEW YORK

Taconic Distillery is a family affair. Paul Coughlin founded the Hudson Valley distillery in 2013. His wife, Carol Ann, runs the on-site bar and develops cocktail recipes. And their three young daughters spend their free time on the bottling line and helping out with tours. (Copper, the family foxhound, provides security.) Like many other distilleries in the state, Taconic takes advantage of New York's farm distillery license, which helps out small producers who use local grains and fruit to make their spirits.

Taconic Founder's Rye

95 percent rye and 5 percent malted barley

AGE No age statement		
ALC/VOL **45**%		
NOSE Lemon, orange peel, iced tea, blackberry jam, marzipan	**MOUTHFEEL** Light to medium	**FINISH** Medium; dark chocolate
GENERAL Easy to drink but not simple—there's a lot going on for what tastes like a very young rye.	**PALATE** Chocolate, orange butter-cream, allspice, toasted grain	
PRICE $$	**RATING**	

Tattersall Distilling

MINNEAPOLIS, MINNESOTA AND RIVER FALLS, WISCONSIN

In 2019, Tattersall teamed up with archivists at the University of Minnesota to resurrect spirits recipes from medieval medicinal texts, beverage alcohol being long thought to have curative properties. Plague water, anyone? It only made a small amount, for an exhibit, but the episode illustrates the creativity at the heart of the distillery, which recently relocated its main production plant to River Falls, Wisconsin (it kept its tasting room in Minneapolis). Tattersall also makes a variety of more contemporary spirits, including gin, vodka, aquavit, rum, and, of course, bourbon and rye.

Tattersall Straight Rye

85 percent rye and 15 percent malted rye

AGE		
2 years old		
ALC/VOL		
50%		

NOSE	MOUTHFEEL	FINISH
Baking spices (mace, in particular), brown sugar, brown butter, cherries, floral	Full	Quite hot, with an underlying note of sweet bread

GENERAL	PALATE	
Almost scotch-like, especially on the nose. This is a big, distinctive, tasty whiskey, but some of the flavors get muddled.	Drying and grain-forward, with fruit cake, and some young-rye herbal notes at mid-palate	
	PRICE	RATING
	$$$	★ ★

Templeton Rye

TEMPLETON, IOWA

Templeton's roots, according to the company, go back to Prohibition, when illegal whiskey made in the town was a speakeasy favorite in Omaha, Chicago, and other Midwestern cities. In 2006 the company began sourcing MGP rye and blending it with a proprietary set of ingredients to make it taste like the Prohibition-era liquid. Templeton built a distillery and intends to release its own whiskey soon.

Templeton 6-Year-Old Rye

95 percent rye and 5 percent malted barley

AGE	**6** years old
ALC/VOL	**45.75**%

NOSE	MOUTHFEEL	FINISH
Dill, orange drink, mint, black licorice, vanilla	Medium	Short; pine

GENERAL	PALATE
An austere and herbal rye, especially on the palate.	Root beer, pine, leather, orange peel

PRICE	RATING
$$	

Thirteenth Colony Distillery

AMERICUS, GEORGIA

Located in southwest Georgia, Thirteenth Colony was the first legal distillery to open in the state since Prohibition, with production beginning in 2009. According to its founders, the company grew out of a conversation about how to make moonshine to give as holiday gifts. The distillery quickly took off, but it has by design remained small and truly small batch, with its whiskeys available in select Southern states but rarely found beyond them.

Thirteenth Colony Southern Rye Whiskey

96 percent rye and 4 percent malted barley; aged in new charred oak barrels with toasted French oak wood spirals

AGE	ALC/VOL
No age statement	**47.5**%

NOSE	MOUTHFEEL	FINISH
Hay, grass, orange candy, wood spices	Light	Quick; dry

GENERAL	PALATE
A refreshing nose, with rye spices that don't overwhelm. It's a good choice for bourbon drinkers. Try it in a Manhattan.	Soft herbal spice, dill, white pepper

PRICE	RATING
$$	★ ★ ★

Three Chord Whiskey

NO LOCATION

Three Chord is a passion project of veteran rocker Neil Giraldo, who played guitar for Pat Benatar (whom he later married), Rick Springfield, and Kenny Loggins, among others. A whiskey fan, Giraldo says he wondered whether the process of blending musical instruments in a band was anything like blending whiskey. The answer, for him, was yes, and Three Chord was born. While Giraldo provides the vision and direction, day-to-day expert direction is offered by Ari Sussman, a veteran craft distiller (he also works for Mammoth Distilling; see page 148).

Three Chord Amplify Rye

95 percent rye and 5 percent malted barley

AGE	No age statement
ALC/VOL	**47.5**%

NOSE	MOUTHFEEL	FINISH
Artificial grape, rubber, potpourri, butyric acid	Light	Brief; nutty

GENERAL	PALATE	
An off-outting whiskey, with an unmistakable whiff of baby vomit on the nose and a palate of mushy cereal.	Feinty, wet grain, amaretto, candy coconut	
	PRICE	RATING
	$$	**NR**

Tincup Whiskey

Jess Graber, a former fireman, was a founding partner of Stranahan's, a Colorado whiskey company focused on single malts. He left the distillery to found Tincup, a sourced brand producing a bourbon–single malt blend, straight bourbon, and rye whiskey.

Tincup Straight Rye

95 percent rye and 5 percent malted barley

AGE	**3** years old
ALC/VOL	**45**%

NOSE	MOUTHFEEL	FINISH
Vegetable garden, black tea, Concord grape, lilac	Light	Medium; chocolate-covered nuts

GENERAL	PALATE	
A square, over-the-plate rye, but the finish lags. There are decent components, but they don't cohere.	Vanilla, treacle, lemon, cinnamon candy, new wood	

PRICE	RATING
$$	★ ★

Tom's Foolery Distillery

BURTON, OHIO

If your name is Tom, then "Tom's Foolery" seems like the perfect name for a distillery. To its founders, Tom and Lianne Herbruck, it is a labor of love; they do much of the work themselves and often fly under the radar of even other Midwestern whiskey fans. The distillery sits on a broad farm halfway between Cleveland and the Pennsylvania border.

Tom's Foolery Bonded Rye

69 percent rye, 27 percent malted rye, and 4 percent malted barley

AGE	
6 years old	

ALC/VOL	
50%	

NOSE	MOUTHFEEL	FINISH
Vanilla creme brûlée, peach, old eraser, wood shavings	Light	Medium; peppermint

GENERAL	PALATE
There are some pleasant elements to this whiskey, but it has youthful quality that detracts, especially in the mouth-pulling tannins on the palate.	Floral, lemon zest, dill, peppermint, popsicle stick, tannic

	PRICE	RATING
	$$	

Town Branch Whiskey

LEXINGTON, KENTUCKY

Town Branch, part of the Lexington Brewing & Distilling Co., is just one part of a transcontinental spirits business. It's a relatively small facility owned by a very large multinational corporation, Alltech, which makes a variety of agricultural products, including, fittingly, yeast (and which also owns a whiskey distillery in Dublin). Alltech was founded by an Irishman named Pearse Lyons, and his Old World preferences are reflected in the distillery. All the whiskey, even the bourbon, is made on a pair of large pot stills built by Forsyths, a famed coppersmith in the Speyside region of Scotland.

Town Branch Straight Rye

55 percent rye, 30 percent corn, and 15 percent malted barley

AGE No age statement		
ALC/VOL **50**%		
NOSE Mushrooms, turmeric, chicken broth, asphalt	**MOUTHFEEL** Full	**FINISH** Medium; leather
GENERAL An oddball, with its nutty, earthy notes, but a pleasing one. A fun sipper of a rye.	**PALATE** Brown butter, pepper, pecan sandy cookie	
	PRICE $$	**RATING**

Treaty Oak Distilling

DRIPPING SPRINGS, TEXAS

Founded in 2006 in Austin, Treaty Oak was only the fourth distillery to open in Texas since the turn of the millenium. A decade later it moved to a larger space in nearby Dripping Springs, but it maintained its connection to the state capital: among other things, its name comes from a 500-year-old tree in the city, under which Stephen F. Austin reportedly signed a treaty outlining the borders of Texas. Its rye is sourced from the Schenley Distillery in Canada.

Treaty Oak Red Handed Rye

53 percent rye, 39 percent corn, and 8 percent malted barley

AGE	ALC/VOL
10 years old	**50**%

NOSE	MOUTHFEEL	FINISH
Rum raisin, vanilla, rubbery, leather, spiced tea	Light to medium	Medium; tannic

GENERAL	PALATE
The palate is young and grain-forward but complex and alluring; it plays to rye's strengths with its grain and vegetal qualities.	Grapefruit, cantaloupe, leather, rum funk, honey

PRICE	RATING
$$$	

Treaty Oak Schenley Reserve Straight Rye

53 percent rye, 39 percent corn, and 8 percent malted barley

AGE
10
years old

ALC/VOL
45%

NOSE
Vanilla, butterscotch, zabaglione, slight herbal liqueur edge

MOUTHFEEL
Full

FINISH
Medium; bittersweet

GENERAL
The palate is nicely balanced between the sharpness of the spices and a dollop of creaminess. A little goes a long way.

PALATE
Cream, coffee, rye bread, wood spices, leather

PRICE
$$$

RATING
★ ★
★

Triple R Rye

GRATON, CALIFORNIA

Produced by Graton Distilling Co., the same Sonoma County distillery that makes Redwood Empire, Triple R stands for Russian River Rye, after the waterway that flows nearby. It's a sourced whiskey, from MGP in Indiana.

Triple R Russian River Straight Rye

95 percent rye and 5 percent malted barley

AGE No age statement		
ALC/VOL **45%**		

NOSE	MOUTHFEEL	FINISH
Grilled papaya, varnish, tobacco ash, oatmeal, biscuits	Light	Short; sandalwood

GENERAL	PALATE	
A bit on the sweet side, but one-dimensional in its structure and flavors. Enjoyable, but not awe-inspiring.	Grilled peach, black tea, lemon, cinnamon bun	
	PRICE **$$**	**RATING**

Two James Spirits

DETROIT, MICHIGAN

Two James is named after the fathers of its two founders, Peter Bailey and David Landrum. Bailey is a scientist, and Landrum is a veteran bartender. Their distillery, located in the Corktown neighborhood of Detroit, was the first to open in the city since Prohibition. As with many distilleries that opened in the early 2010s, master distiller David Pickerell served as its midwife, consultant, and secret sauce in human form for the first several years.

Two James Spirits Catcher's Straight Rye

100 percent rye

AGE		
No age statement		
ALC/VOL		
49.4%		

NOSE	MOUTHFEEL	FINISH
Rubber, butterscotch, dark chocolate, grilled tropical fruit	Light	Medium; roasted nuts

GENERAL	PALATE	
This is a hard whiskey to love—the rubber on the nose and palate is a turnoff. But the effort is worth it, because there is a lot hidden in its depths.	Rubber, lime pith, vegetal, tobacco	
	PRICE	**RATING**
	$$$	★★

Union Horse Distilling Co.

LENEXA, KANSAS

Around 2009, the four Garcia siblings were sitting around their kitchen table, talking about their mutual love of whiskey. It didn't take long for them to decide to give it a shot themselves—and Union Horse was born. All four are still there: Eric is the general manager, Patrick is the master distiller, Damian does marketing, and Mary runs special events. Known as Dark Horse until 2015, Union Horse makes vodka and white dog, as well as bourbon, rye, and a four-grain whiskey called Rolling Standard.

Union Horse Reunion Straight Rye

100 percent rye

AGE		No age statement
ALC/VOL		**46.5%**

NOSE	MOUTHFEEL	FINISH
Grilled papaya, varnish, tobacco ash, oatmeal, biscuits	Full	Medium; tobacco

GENERAL	PALATE
Like a rye made in Armagnac—wonderful old barrel notes, with notes of raisin and rum. But the rye backbone remains, with spices and herbs.	Char, leather, tobacco, raisins, rum, cardamom, vanilla

PRICE	RATING
$$	

Van Brunt Stillhouse

BROOKLYN, NEW YORK

Located in the Brooklyn neighborhood of Red Hook and just around the corner from the Widow Jane distillery (page 236), Van Brunt is one of the oldest operating distilleries in New York, getting its start in 2013. It remains small, even by New York standards, though its size allows its owners, Daric Schlesselman and Sarah Ludington, to play around with finishes and mash bills in a way that a larger craft distillery might not be able to do.

Van Brunt Stillhouse Empire Rye

75 percent rye and 25 percent malted barley

AGE		
No age statement		

ALC/VOL
57.5%

NOSE	MOUTHFEEL	FINISH
Apple juice, pencil shavings, pine, mint, candied lemon peel	Light	Medium; herbal and chocolate

GENERAL	PALATE	
Serviceable and solid. Not a memorable rye but it does what it needs to do.	Cocoa, toasted grain, nutty, mint, slightly tannic	

PRICE	RATING
$$	★★★

Very Olde St. Nick

BARDSTOWN, KENTUCKY

Marci Palatella is one of the O.G. figures in the prehistory of the American whiskey renaissance. She saw, starting in the 1980s, how undervalued American bourbon and rye had become, and that stunning barrels could be had for nothing. Like Julian Van Winkle III and Even Kulsveen, of the Willett Distillery, she snatched them up, then bottled them for export or limited domestic sale, under the Olde St. Nick label. In 2016 she opened the Preservation Distillery in Bardstown, where her team makes a small amount of whiskey on site and continues to bottle sourced barrels as well.

Very Olde St. Nick Cask Strength Summer Rye

Undisclosed mash bill

AGE	ALC/VOL
No age statement	**59.2**%
	Varies

NOSE	MOUTHFEEL	FINISH
Maple, dark fruit, Demerara sugar, lemon, cloves	Full	Long; nutty bitterness

GENERAL	PALATE	
Lot of amplitude and difference on the nose, with gripping aromas redolent of spicy old rum. Exquisite.	Vanilla, lemon curd, toast, almonds, cola, dark fruits	

	PRICE	RATING
	$$$$	★ ★ ★ ★

Very Olde Saint Nick Ancient Cask 8-Year-Old Rye

Undisclosed mash bill

AGE

8
years old

ALC/VOL

42.3%

NOSE

Lavender, lemon balm, verbena, thyme, dill

MOUTHFEEL

Light

FINISH

Short; rum

GENERAL

This has a distinct rum quality to it that sets it apart from other ryes but doesn't necessarily elevate it. Otherwise, it's solid but unremarkable.

PALATE

Autumnal, pumpkin spice, chocolate, leather, rum

PRICE

RATING

Virgil Kaine Lowcountry Whiskey Co.

CHARLESTON, SOUTH CAROLINA

"Virgil Caine is the name, and I served on the Danville train"—so begins "The Night They Drove Ole Dixie Down," one of The Band's greatest hits. Caine, a fictional train conductor and folk hero, also lends his name (with a slightly different spelling) to the Virgil Kaine distillery. The company gets its whiskey from undisclosed sources, though it finishes and infuses some of it on its own, including a ginger-infused bourbon.

Virgil Kaine Robber Baron Rye

95 percent rye and 5 percent malted barley

AGE
No age statement

ALC/VOL
45.5%

NOSE
Rose, lime, coconut, pear, cherry, sawdust

MOUTHFEEL
Full

FINISH
Short; cinnamon

GENERAL
Well-crafted but it drinks a little young. It's heavy on the florals and fruit, but missing the darker notes of red-line extraction.

PALATE
Juicy Fruit, cinnamon, malt, lemon, key lime pie

PRICE
$$

RATING

Wheel Horse Whiskey

NO LOCATION

Owensboro, Kentucky, was once a hotspot for bourbon distilling, but today there is just one game in town, the Green River Distillery. Along with its own label, Green River contract-distills for several brands, chief among them Wheel Horse, a bourbon and rye whiskey owned by Latitude Beverage, out of Boston. It's worth noting that while Green River produces several whiskies using its parent company's TerrePURE rapid-maturation technology, Wheel Horse isn't one of them—this is properly aged whiskey.

Wheel Horse Straight Rye

95 percent rye and 5 percent malted barley

AGE	ALC/VOL
No age statement	**50.5**%

NOSE	MOUTHFEEL	FINISH
Grilled papaya, barbecue, herbes de Provence, black tea	Full	Medium; caramel

GENERAL	PALATE
Candied, but it is balanced with tannin and some char-like notes. It comes off more like a malt than a rye.	Sweet tea, preserved plums, lemon pith, cocoa

PRICE	RATING
$	★★

Whip Saw Rye

NO LOCATION

The Splinter Group emerged from the shared vision of Bob Cabral and John Wilkinson, two California winemakers who loved whiskey and wanted to recast it in their own terms. The company buys mature whiskey, then finishes it in a variety of California wine barrels, all made from French oak.

Whip Saw Rye

6 percent rye, 21 percent corn, and 3 percent malted barley; finished in wine casks

AGE No age statement		
ALC/VOL **45**%		

NOSE	MOUTHFEEL	FINISH
Demerara sugar, bittersweet chocolate, amaretto, date nut bread	Full	Medium; rum

GENERAL	PALATE
Strong rum overtones, including a pleasant rubbery tinge on the palate. Think of rum raisin more than straight rum.	Raisins, rubber, chalk, coconut, roasted pecans, amaretto

PRICE	RATING
$$	★★

WhistlePig Distillery

SHOREHAM, VERMONT

For much of its existence, WhistlePig was only nominally an American whiskey. Its founder, Raj Bhakta, and consultant David Pickerell bought most its whiskey from Alberta, Canada, running the show from a farm in central Vermont. Pickerell passed away in 2018 and Bhakta sold out soon after, leaving the company in new hands. It has since begun releasing whiskey made on site, as well as whiskey sourced from other distilleries in the United States.

WhistlePig Double Malt 18-Year-Old Straight Rye

	AGE **18** years old

79 percent rye, 15 percent malted rye, and 6 percent malted barley; finished in Vermont oak

ALC/VOL 46%

NOSE	MOUTHFEEL	FINISH
Gently floral, subtle baking spices, savory, orchard fruit	Light	Long, creamy

GENERAL	PALATE
A delicate, elegant whiskey that sits on the line between rye and Bas-Armagnac. Outstanding.	Baking spices, rancio, vanilla, sandalwood

PRICE	RATING
$$$$	★ ★ ★ ★

WhistlePig 15-Year-Old Estate Oak–Aged Straight Rye

	AGE **15** years old

100 percent rye; finished in Vermont oak

ALC/VOL 46%

NOSE	MOUTHFEEL	FINISH
Maple, spice box, spent coffee grounds, pine	Light	Persistent; pine

GENERAL	PALATE
It has a pleasing, surprising tartness, but it lacks depth and nuance.	Red Hots, dried pineapple, orange bitters, pine resin

PRICE	RATING
$$$$	★ ★

WhistlePig Piggyback Rye

100 percent rye

AGE	
6 years old	

ALC/VOL
48.23%

NOSE	MOUTHFEEL	FINISH
Cocoa, orange, key lime pie, mint, fresh cut flower stems	Light	Medium; leather and spice

GENERAL	PALATE
Youthfully elegant, with verve and spice toward the finish. It could shine with more age.	Grain, bergamot, lemon squares, lime zest, vanilla

PRICE	RATING
$$	

WhistlePig Old World Rye

100 percent rye; finished in madeira, Sauternes, and port casks

AGE	
12 years old	

ALC/VOL
43%

NOSE	MOUTHFEEL	FINISH
Orange compote, cola, candied almonds, candied violets	Light to medium	Short; fruity

GENERAL	PALATE
Refreshing and light, with some depth. The nose outshines the palate in the end though.	Black pepper, herbal tea, mint, dill, anise, floral perfume

PRICE	RATING
$$$$	

WhistlePig Farmstock Rye

RYE CROP NO. 003

100 percent rye; a blend of house-distilled and sourced whiskey

AGE	ALC/VOL
3 years old	**50.5**%

NOSE	MOUTHFEEL	FINISH
Orange drink, cinnamon, musky oak, lemon	Full	Short; bitter

GENERAL	PALATE
It's one-dimensional but nonetheless pleasant, especially as it perks up at the mid-palate. What you might call a sessionable whiskey.	Cola, black pepper, orange cream, wood smoke

PRICE	RATING
$$$	

Whistlepig 10-Year-Old Small Batch Rye

100 percent rye

AGE	ALC/VOL
10 years old	**50**%

NOSE	MOUTHFEEL	FINISH
Darkly floral (think dandelions and chamomile), with nutmeg and root beer	Medium	A short, spicy kick in the butt

GENERAL	PALATE
A solid whiskey with enough surprises to keep it interesting. It would make a nice mixer, and it's fun to drink neat.	Big and sweet, with a rye oomph mid-palate; there's malt, honey, cherry, and blond tobacco

PRICE	RATING
$$$	

Widow Jane Distillery

BROOKLYN, NEW YORK

Lisa Wicker didn't found Widow Jane, but since taking the reins in 2019, she has been its brains and heart. The distillery had struggled before she arrived, but under her direction it has started to release both exciting young bourbons and ryes and blends of older, sourced whiskeys. While much of Widow Jane's whiskey is sourced, every bottle is proofed with water from the Rosendale Mines, about 100 miles north of Brooklyn. Their ryes are aged in used barrels and/or barrels made from something other than oak, which according to federal regulations makes them technically not "rye" whiskey, but "whiskey distilled from a rye mash."

Widow Jane Oak & Applewood Aged Whiskey Distilled from a Rye Mash

Undisclosed blend of rye and barley; aged in oak and applewood casks

AGE	ALC/VOL
No age statement	**45.5**%

NOSE	MOUTHFEEL	FINISH
Beeswax, orange oil, acetone, white grapes	Full	Short; spicy

GENERAL	PALATE	
It's hard to get much out of this. Despite a surprisingly round mouthfeel, it shows only faint wisps of whiskey character, let alone rye.	Honey, grain, ethanol, grape skin, apple	

	PRICE	RATING
	$$	★

Widow Jane American Oak Aged Whiskey Distilled from a Rye Mash

Undisclosed blend of rye and barley; aged in a once-used bourbon barrel

AGE
No age statement

ALC/VOL
45.5%

NOSE
Herbaceous, marigolds, red licorice, ginger

MOUTHFEEL
Medium

FINISH
Short, with citrus and black pepper

GENERAL
A well-built if unremarkable whiskey.

PALATE
Ginger, cough syrup, bitter chocolate, cherries

PRICE
$$

RATING
★★

Wigle Whiskey

PITTSBURGH, PENNSYLVANIA

Wigle is the brainchild of Alex and Meredith Meyer Grelli, who founded the Pittsburgh distillery in 2012 in the city's Strip District, a hub for tech startups and R&D labs. Though they work with liquid, not computer chips, the Grellis are right at home: They are fierce advocates for the resurgence of western Pennsylvania rye, and they insist that whiskey made in the region, with local grains, has a unique terroir. It's a claim they supported with the Terroir Project, in which they distilled rye from Canada and two regions in the United States to demonstrate the differences in flavor in the resulting whiskey. (The name Wigle, by the way, comes from a central figure in the Whiskey Rebellion, which took place nearby.)

Wigle Kilted Rye

95 percent rye and 5 percent malted barley; finished in ex-peated scotch quarter casks

AGE No age statement		
ALC/VOL **56%**		
NOSE Musty, earthy, dried mint, cedar	**MOUTHFEEL** Light to medium	**FINISH** Medium; cigar tobacco
GENERAL Consistent and a bit simple, but well done and quite pleasing.	**PALATE** Spiced cherry, black tea, cocoa powder, vanilla	
PRICE **$$$**	**RATING**	

Wigle Deep Cut Bottled-in-Bond Rye

Undisclosed blend of rye and malted barley

AGE	ALC/VOL
5 years old	**50**%

NOSE	MOUTHFEEL	FINISH
Maraschino cherry, vanilla, rose, peach, bitters	Light to medium	Short; pine

GENERAL	PALATE
It opens with some weird, dissonant notes, but by the finish it resolves itself into a classic rye profile.	Cedar, chai, rye bread, butterscotch, club soda

PRICE	RATING
$$$	

Wigle Single Barrel Straight Rye

68 percent rye, 18 percent wheat, and 14 percent malted barley

AGE	ALC/VOL
4 years old	**50**%

NOSE	MOUTHFEEL	FINISH
Raw oak, butterscotch, orange drink, honey, linen	Medium	Medium; mint and fudge

GENERAL	PALATE
An uneasy array of potent flavors that are at odds with one another.	Hops, musty, cocoa powder, grain mash

PRICE	RATING
$$$	

Wigle Pennsylvania Straight Rye

68 percent rye, 18 percent wheat, and 14 percent malted barley

AGE
2
years old

ALC/VOL
42%

NOSE	MOUTHFEEL	FINISH
Flintstones vitamins, bergamot, potpourri, rye toast	Medium	Lengthy; pepper

GENERAL	PALATE
Unbalanced, with too much emphasis on the grainy character of the palate, which shuts out everything else.	Caramel, toasted grain, Red Hots, citrus pith

PRICE
$$

RATING

Wild Turkey Distillery

LAWRENCEBURG, KENTUCKY

Jimmy Russell started working at Wild Turkey in 1954, and his son Eddie joined him in 1981. Together they have over 100 years' experience making whiskey, most of it as master distiller and master distiller emeritus, though the distinction is murky. They share duties, and the same vision for the distillery. Jimmy and Eddie have guided Wild Turkey through whiskey's ups and downs, keeping a steady ship with its 101-proof bourbon and rye offerings while venturing the occasional, well-thought-out innovation. Among those innovations is the Russell's Reserve line, which, although it uses the same mash bill as core Wild Turkey, is aged and blended to produce a softer, more approachable—and more cocktail-friendly—whiskey.

Russell's Reserve Straight Rye

51 percent rye, 37 percent corn, and 12 percent malted barley

AGE	
6	
years old	

ALC/VOL	
45%	

NOSE	MOUTHFEEL	FINISH
Butterscotch, raisins, Concord grape, varnish, almonds	Light	Long and dry

GENERAL	PALATE
This is an expressive older rye that balances the persistent grain influence with the effects of years in a barrel.	Plum, orange soda, aspirin, Concord grape, chocolate

PRICE	RATING
$$	

Wild Turkey 101 Straight Rye

51 percent rye, 37 percent corn, and 12 percent malted barley

AGE	
No age statement	

ALC/VOL	
50.5%	

NOSE	MOUTHFEEL	FINISH
Orange, vanilla, menthol, tobacco, dill, iced tea	Light to medium	Short; cocoa

GENERAL	PALATE
Quite fruity, this one. It loosens and improves with a few drops of water. But it's also punching below its weight.	Cocoa, orange syrup, grapefruit, toasted nuts, black tea

PRICE	RATING
$$	

Wild Turkey Master's Keep Cornerstone Rye

51 percent rye, 37 percent corn, and 12 percent malted barley

AGE
9
years old

ALC/VOL
54.5%

NOSE	MOUTHFEEL	FINISH
Strawberries, vanilla, pralines, blackberries	Medium	Long, with citrus and hot pepper

GENERAL	PALATE
Delicious, balanced, complex, and rewarding. Despite the proof it doesn't need water. Savory but with surprising fruit notes.	Sweet on the entry, with cherry cobbler and dark chocolate, resolving into espresso and citrus

PRICE
$$$$

RATING
★★
★★

Wild Turkey Rare Breed Barrel Proof Rye

AGE
No age statement

ALC/VOL
56.1%

51 percent rye, 37 percent corn, and 12 percent malted barley

NOSE	MOUTHFEEL	FINISH
Black tea, rye bread, cinnamon, caramel	Medium	Long; spicy

GENERAL	PALATE
An expertly crafted, versatile whiskey that hits all the conventional notes but still bears the Wild Turkey imprint.	Caramel, mint, oak char, French vanilla

PRICE
$$$

RATING
★★
★

Wilderness Trail Distillery

DANVILLE, KENTUCKY

Wilderness Trail is one of the largest distilleries to open during Kentucky's whiskey renaissance. It was founded by Shane Baker and Pat Heist, two scientists who met playing in a metal band and decided to go into business together as fermentation consultants. After several years working with dozens of whiskey distilleries, they decided to open their own. The result is Wilderness Trail, a sprawling, state-of-the-art facility near Danville. Along with Wilderness Trail's own brand of bourbon and rye, the distillery also contract-distills for a variety of clients, with innovative recipes made possible by a state-of-the-art fermentation lab located on site.

Wilderness Trail Settlers Select Single Barrel Straight Rye

BARREL NO. ISIS19D

56 percent rye, 33 percent corn, and 11 percent malted barley

AGE	No age statement
ALC/VOL	**60**% *Varies* (Barrel Proof)

NOSE	MOUTHFEEL	FINISH
Fudge, cherry cola, candied orange peel, sweet tobacco, celery seed	Full	Long,; dark fruits

GENERAL	PALATE	
Rich and complicated, it benefits from adding water and may be a rare rye that should have been bottled at a lower proof (the sample tasted was 60% ABV). Still, it's delicious.	Amaretto, mint, licorice, dark cherry, caraway seed	
	PRICE	RATING
	$$	★ ★ ★ ★

Willett Distillery

BARDSTOWN, KENTUCKY

Willett is responsible for some of the most sought-after, legendary bottles of American whiskey ever produced. Whiskeys like LeNell's Red Hook Rye, the original Black Maple Hill, and Kentucky Vintage were all bottled at Willett from its vast stock of barrels that its owners, the Kulsveen family, had purchased from other distilleries. In 2005, the distillery created Willett Family Estate, a single-barrel bottling program; customers interested in buying their own barrel could pick from the extensive collection of aging whiskey, which the distillery would then bottle. Again, Willett created legends, with bottlings like Doug's Green Ink and Velvet Glove, all labeled with the distinctive Willett family crest. Finally, in 2012, Willett restarted its distilling program, with its rye whiskey as its new flagship offering.

Willett Family Estate 4-Year-Old Straight Rye

Undisclosed mash bill

AGE	
4 years old	

ALC/VOL
55%

NOSE	MOUTHFEEL	FINISH
Herbal, black licorice, savory, putty, sarsaparilla	Full	Long; herbaceous

GENERAL	PALATE
A genuine expression of rye spirit that's unique and full of character. A rye drinker's rye.	Dill, vinegar, barbecue sauce, root beer candy, celery

PRICE	RATING
$$$	

William Wolf Whiskey

NO LOCATION

William Wolf is a curious whiskey: It uses American spirits, but it is bottled in the Netherlands. The brand is best known for its pecan-infused whiskey, but its producers offer a bourbon and a rye expression as well.

William Wolf Rye

100 percent rye

AGE	No age statement
ALC/VOL	**46**%

NOSE	MOUTHFEEL	FINISH
Hops, pine, asphalt, nutmeg, sage brush	Medium	Medium; bitter

GENERAL	PALATE	
What the desert smells like after a rain. It's all about aggressive, youthful wood notes. Not off-putting, but it but it needs to chill out.	Concord grape, dark citrus, aggressive wood, potpourri	
	PRICE $$	**RATING** ★★

Winchester Rye

NO LOCATION

Like Copper Pony, Winchester is a brand carried primarily at Total Wine & More and produced by Green River Spirits (though not distilled at its Owensboro, Kentucky, distillery). The South Carolina–based company buys young whiskey, then puts it through its patented TerrePURE process, which it claims can add several years of age to the whiskey almost immediately.

Winchester Rye

Undisclosed mash bill

AGE		
No age statement		

ALC/VOL
45%

NOSE	MOUTHFEEL	FINISH
Unctuous, Bit-O-Honey, tobacco barn, chicken noodle soup	Light	Medium; Juicy Fruit

GENERAL	PALATE
The palate opens quite sweetly, then dries and darkens. Interesting, even tasty notes, but it lacks enough vividness and intensity to carry the day.	Sugary pie crust, fruit tea, cinnamon, nutmeg, Red Hots

PRICE	RATING
$	

Woodford Reserve Distillery

VERSAILLES, KENTUCKY

Founded by Brown-Forman in 1995, Woodford Reserve is one of the original distilleries of the Kentucky whiskey renaissance. Although it sits in the heart of Kentucky bourbon country, it could easily be mistaken for a single malt scotch distillery, from its Highlands-inflected architecture to its pot stills, manufactured by Forsyths, the famed Scottish coppersmiths. It is best known for its iconic bourbon, a blend of whiskey made on site and at Brown-Forman's large distillery in Louisville. Woodford Reserve rye is a relatively recent addition to its lineup, and it carries the same elegant, full-flavored profile of the distillery's flagship bourbon. Woodford also offers a number of limited and distillery-only expressions, including the occasional rye.

Woodford Reserve Straight Rye

53 percent rye, 33 percent corn, and 14 percent malted barley

AGE	No age statement	
ALC/VOL	**45.2**%	
NOSE	MOUTHFEEL	FINISH
Lemon candy, cola, dill, pine furniture, coconut	Light	Short; espresso
GENERAL	PALATE	
A classic, full-bodied rye, suggesting itself for an after-dinner drink alongside a slice of coffee cake.	Leather, toasted nuts, coconut cake, root beer	
	PRICE	RATING
	$$	★★★

Woodinville Whiskey Co.

WOODINVILLE, WASHINGTON

Like Hillrock Estate and WhistlePig, Woodinville is a legacy project of the legendary Dave Pickerell, who left his job as the master distiller at Maker's Mark to become the "Johnny Appleseed" of craft whiskey. He helped countless distilleries get their start, and Woodinville was one of his greatest successes. Located outside Seattle, the distillery was founded by two friends, Orlin Sorensen and Brett Carlile. From the beginning, they sourced all their grain from a single, nearby farm, and distilled it on a custom made 1,320-gallon pot still. Luxury group Moët Hennessy acquired Woodinville in 2017

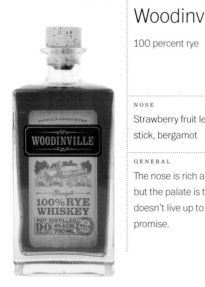

Woodinville Straight Rye

100 percent rye

AGE	No age statement

ALC/VOL
45%

NOSE	MOUTHFEEL	FINISH
Strawberry fruit leather, Popsicle stick, bergamot	Light	Short; tannic

GENERAL	PALATE	
The nose is rich and promising, but the palate is too thin and doesn't live up to its olfactory promise.	Cantaloupe, citrus, linseed oil, tea leaves	

PRICE	RATING
$$	★★

Yellow Rose Distilling

HOUSTON, TEXAS

Yellow Rose calls itself the first whiskey made in Houston since Prohibition, which sounds niche until you remember that at 4 million people and change, Houston has a larger population than many American states. The distillery began by sourcing its products and blending them, but in recent years it has moved to bottling its own whiskey.

Yellow Rose Rye   BATCH 19-4

95 percent rye and 5 percent malted barley

AGE	No age statement
ALC/VOL	**45**%

NOSE	MOUTHFEEL	FINISH
Celery, mixed nuts, grain silo, Lemon Joy dish soap	Light to medium	Long; spearmint

GENERAL	PALATE	
Uncomplex, vivacious, youthful—a decently made young rye. Easy-drinking if not especially interesting.	Grass, raw peanuts, lemon, spearmint	
	PRICE	RATING
	$$	

Acknowledgments

This book, the third in an ongoing series, began in a conversation. I have never not thoroughly enjoyed working with George Scott, and so when he suggested that we follow up our book on single malt scotch with a book about American rye whiskey, it didn't take me a second to say, "I'm in." Of course, it took us more than that—much, much more than that—to get the project rolling, thanks to Covid, but it came to fruition because of his dogged commitment. At one point, we were running our tasting panel virtually, a feat made possible by an even greater effort on George's part—every few weeks he would pour and label hundreds of small samples, then drive them around New York City and even mail a set to Reid Mitenbuler, in Los Angeles. Cheers to you, my friend.

Speaking of Reid, he and the rest of the tasting panel—Kurt, Susannah, Elizabeth, Liza, Pradeep, and Josh—deserve Politburo-length standing ovations for their patience and commitment to our yearlong digital slog. I hope they enjoyed our weekly gatherings as much as I did.

My special thanks go to all the distillers and public relations professionals who helped me and George track down bottles to sample. One of the great things about my odd choice of profession is that distillers don't seem to find it odd at all—in fact, I have never felt anything other than wholly welcomed by a community I know very little about. And while it's true that they have every good reason to be nice to a guy who wants to shower flowery kindnesses over them, I've covered enough parts of the world to know that's not always the case.

George and I spent a chilly, soggy morning trooping around southwestern Pennsylvania with Sam Komlenic and Aaron Hollis, looking at the origins and ruins of the state's rye whiskey industry. Their knowledge is matched only by their generosity.

And as always, I reserve my biggest thanks for Joanna, Talia and Elliot. Though I don't always have the words to express it, and while it's not always obvious, I wrote this book for you.

Further reading

Bryson, Lew. *Tasting Whiskey: An Insider's Guide to the Unique Pleasures of the World's Finest Spirits.* North Adams: Storey Publishing, 2014.

Carson, Gerald. *The Social History of Bourbon*. Lexington: The University Press of Kentucky, 1963.

Cecil, Sam K. *Bourbon: The Evolution of Kentucky Whiskey.* Nashville: Turner Publishing, 2010.

Cowdery, Charles K. *Bourbon, Straight: The Uncut and Unfiltered Story of American Whiskey.* Chicago: Made and Bottled in Kentucky, 2004.

Crowgey, Henry G. *Kentucky Bourbon: The Early Years of Whiskey Making.* Lexington: The University Press of Kentucky, 2008.

DeVoto, Bernard. *The Hour: A Cocktail Manifesto*. Boston: Houghton Mifflin, 1951.

Meyer, Mark and Meredith Meyer Grelli. *The Whiskey Rebellion and the Rebirth of Rye: A Pittsburgh Story*. Cleveland: Belt Publishing, 2017.

Mitenbuler, Reid. *Bourbon Empire: The Past and Future of America's Whiskey.* New York: Penguin, 2016.

Rorabaugh, W. J. *The Alcoholic Republic: An American Tradition.* New York: Oxford University Press, 1979.

Taylor, Richard. *The Great Crossing: A Historic Journey to Buffalo Trace Distillery*. Frankfort: Buffalo Trace Distillery, 2002.

Thompson, Wright. *Pappyland: A Story of Family, Fine Bourbon, and the Things That Last*. New York: Penguin Press, 2020.

Veach, Michael R. *Kentucky Bourbon Whiskey: An American Heritage.* Lexington: The University Press of Kentucky, 2013.

Wondrich, David and Noah Rothbaum. *The Oxford Companion to Spirits and Cocktails.* New York: Oxford University Press, 2021.

Glossary of Terms

ALCOHOL BY VOLUME (ABV): The amount of alcohol in whiskey as a percentage of the total volume.

ANGELS' SHARE: The amount of liquid that escapes, as vapor, though a barrel as it ages. Rule of thumb says it should be about 5 percent a year, but that can vary based on air pressure and humidity.

BARREL: All straight rye whiskey made in the United States must be aged in new, charred oak containers, which in practice means barrels. The standard size is 53 gallons, but they can be found as small as 5 gallons. All barrels are made with curved staves, bounded by steel hoops, and fitted with round wood heads at each end.

BEER: The goopy sludge that results from fermenting a grain mash. It's not literally beer, but it's close to it.

BOTTLED IN BOND: Essentially a government seal of approval. According to the Bottled-in-Bond Act of 1897, a whiskey that has been a) made at one distillery in b) a single distilling season, and c) aged for at least four years in d) a warehouse bonded by the U.S. government, then e) bottled at 100 proof, may be labeled "Bottled in Bond." The name carries less weight today, when all alcohol is tightly regulated, but at the time the designation gave distillers who followed its rules a leg up over less-reputable competition.

BOURBON: Federal law requires that bourbon be made with 51-percent corn in its mash bill, come off the still at no more than 160 proof, and go into a charred, new oak barrel at no more than 125 proof. The vast majority of whiskey made in American is bourbon.

CHAR: The burnt inside of a barrel, achieved by briefly setting the interior on fire. Doing so creates a filter to remove unwanted compounds from a whiskey, and it caramelizes the sugars trapped deeper in the wood.

COLUMN STILL: The dominant style of still in the United States. Developed in Ireland in the early nineteenth century, it is a hollow column in which steam is pumped into the bottom.

Fermented mash is poured in from higher up the column, and as the two meet, the steam strips out the alcohol in the mash, carrying it to the top and out to a condenser. Most column stills have a number of perforated plates inside them; the arrangement of the plates affects how much water, alcohol, and other compounds are extracted. A column still is usually paired with a small pot still called a doubler, which purifies the distillate further.

DISTILLATION: The process of separating out the components of a liquid, usually by the application of heat. In whiskey, a fermented mash is distilled to separate out much of the water and unwanted compounds from the alcohol.

DOUBLER: A pot-shaped still, smaller than the primary column or pot, used to concentrate or refine alcohol further after an initial distillation.

ESTER: Fermentation, distillation, and maturation yield a dizzying number of chemical compounds, including hundreds of esters produced by the combination of acids and alcohols. Esters are critical in creating flavors, aromas, and textures in whiskey.

HEADS: The very first liquid to come off a still. It contains various compounds and alcohols that, while not desirable in a distillate per se, are typically added back into the still to be redistilled.

HEARTS: The middle portion of a distillation run. The hearts contain almost pure ethanol and the most desirable flavor compounds in the distillate.

MALT: A grain, usually barley but sometimes rye (and in some rare cases, corn), that has been allowed to germinate, but has been dried out before fully sprouting. The process activates enzymes that convert complex starches in the grain into yeast-friendly sugar. In the United States, malt is typically used solely for this purpose, instead of for flavor.

MASH: The sludge of cooked milled grain and water that, after pitching in yeast, becomes distiller's beer.

MASH BILL: Essentially, a whiskey's "recipe." The typical

American rye whiskey has at least two grains in its mash bill—rye and malted barley—though some contain wheat or corn as well, or all four.

NON-AGE STATEMENT (NAS): A whiskey without an age on the label. Still, a discerning drinker can identify some clues. If it is labeled "straight," the whiskey is at least two years old, and federal law dictates it should include an age statement if under four years. If it says straight and there is no age statement, it's at least four years old.

NON-DISTILLING PRODUCER (NDP): These days it seems like most whiskey companies don't make what they sell. Instead, they either contract with distillers to produce a custom mash bill or simply buy whiskey and bottle it. Being an NDP is neither a good nor a bad thing, though there are very good NDPs and very anonymous, if not outright bad, NDPs as well.

POT STILL: The concept of the pot still has been around since the invention of distilling. It is essentially a pot with a sealed conical lid on top, with a metal spout running out of it. A fermented liquid is placed inside and heat is applied to the bottom, so that the liquid vaporizes. A skilled technician can watch the distilled liquid come off the still and decide what to keep, what to redistill, and what to toss away.

PROOF: Like alcohol by volume, the measure of the alcoholic content of a liquor. In the United States, the number is arrived at by doubling the percentage of alcohol in the spirit. The term comes from a time before the invention of alcohol meters and hydrometers. Grains of gunpowder were mixed with a small amount of spirit; if they could be set on fire, then that was considered "proof" that the liquid was about 50-percent alcohol.

RICKHOUSE: The warehouse where whiskey is matured. In the United States, most of them are multistory and made of wood, though brick, metal, and even concrete examples can be found.

RYE: A grain, a whiskey, and the subject of the book. Rye grain originated in the Euphrates Valley, migrated to northern Europe, and arrived in North America with the earliest European settlers. A hearty grass grown as often as a cover crop as it is for food, rye was also among the first grains used to produce whiskey in Colonial America. Rye whiskey was once the most popular alcoholic beverage on the East Coast, but it disappeared after Prohibition—only to come roaring back in the twenty-first century.

SOUR MASH: The process of adding spent mash, called the backset, left from one distillation into a new batch. Sour refers to the slightly acidic character of the spent mash, which is beneficial for fermentation; it does not make the whiskey sour.

STRAIGHT WHISKEY: The subject of strict federal rules. The important thing is that it is at least two years old—four years if there is no age statement. It also must be aged in new, charred oak barrels, and cannot contain any additives other than water. Any type of whiskey—bourbon, rye, wheat, what have you—can be straight.

SWEET MASH: The opposite of sour mash. All the yeast and grain are fresh, with no backset added.

TAILS: The last cut of a distillation run, containing various trace compounds and alcohols, as well as some ethanol. A distiller collects the tails and may discard or redistill them.

TOASTING: The process of heating, but not burning, the inside of a barrel to concentrate compounds deep in the staves.

VARIETAL: A subtype of a species, somewhat akin to breeds among dogs and cats. Rye, for example, the species Secale cereale, has dozens of varietals, including Abruzzi and Rosen, both increasingly popular among craft distillers.

YEAST: Nothing happens without yeast, the voracious microscopic flora that, when added to a sugary liquid, consumes the sweet and emits alcohol, until the amount of the latter gets so high that it kills the yeast. Who said whiskey isn't violent?

Risen's Top Ryes

Taste is subjective, of course, but some whiskeys are simply better than others, and a few truly stand out. Below are our favorites, broken down into four categories.

Top Ten Ryes   *These are the whiskeys that absolutely floored us.*

1. Michter's 25-Year-Old Rye **2.** Thomas H. Handy Straight Rye **3.** Kentucky Owl Straight Rye (Batch 4)
4. Lock, Stock & Barrel 18-Year-Old Rye **5.** Michter's 10-Year-Old Rye **6.** Old Carter Straight Rye (Batch 6
7. Van Winkle Family Reserve Rye **8.** Kentucky Peerless Barrel Proof Rye
9. Whistlepig 10-Year-Old Rye **10.** Kooper Family Barrel Reserve Rye

Top Craft Ryes

Younger whiskeys from newer distilleries, they're bottles to seek and producers to watch.

1. Dad's Hat Rye Finished in Port Wine Barrels
2. Distillery 291 Colorado Rye
3. New Riff Bottled-In-Bond Rye
4. Kings County Empire Straight Rye
5. McKenzie Rye
6. New Liberty Fortunato's Fate Rye
7. Starlight Old Rickhouse Straight Rye
8. Reservoir Rye
9. Koval Single Barrel Rye
10. Stoll & Wolfe Pennsylvania Rye

Top Gift Ryes

Great whiskeys and crowd-pleasers to boot, give these to rye fans and skeptics alike.

1. Blue Run Golden Straight Rye
2. High West A Midwinter's Night Dram
3. Jack Daniel's Single Barrel Straight Rye
4. Russell's Reserve Straight Rye
5. Pinhook Straight Rye

Top Value Ryes

Great whiskey doesn't have to be expensive, as these ryes can attest.

1. Clyde May's 8-Year-Old Straight Rye
2. James E. Pepper 1776 Straight Rye
3. Old Forester Straight Rye
4. Old Overholt Bottled-in-Bond
5. Wild Turkey 101 Rye

The Tasting Panel

Clay Risen is a reporter at *The New York Times* and the author of *Bourbon: The Story of Kentucky Whiskey*, *The Impossible Collection of Whiskey*, *Single Malt: A Guide to the Whiskies of Scotland*, and the bestselling *American Whiskey, Bourbon and Rye: A Guide to the Nation's Favorite Spirit*.

Susannah Skiver Barton, a seasoned blind taster and critic, writes about whiskies and spirits from around the world. She's a certified spirits specialist and the winner of the Alan Lodge Young International Drinks Writer Award. More at susannahskiverbarton.com.

Elizabeth Emmons fell in love with whisky upon her first sip of Laphroaig fourteen years ago and has since had an avid interest in the history and craft of the spirit. Elizabeth is a contributing writer to the online magazine "The Whiskey Reviewer," and is an active member of various whiskey and spirit tasting groups and judging panels in New York City.

Josh Feldman is a well-regarded whiskey blogger known for detailed historical essays at "The Coopered Tot" (cooperedtot.com). A fixture in the New York whiskey scene, Josh leads tasting events and presents about whiskey history. He works and has also led events at The Morgan Library, where he is network administrator.

Kurt Maitland started his whiskey journey with drams of Jameson in college and has been exploring the wider world of whisky/whiskey ever since. He currently is the deputy editor of the popular "Whiskey Reviewer" website, the curator of the Manhattan Whiskey Club, and the author of two books on cocktails: *Drink* and *The Infused Cocktail Handbook*.

Pradeep Massand is the owner of Valley Stream Wine & Liquor. After a full career in information technology, Pradeep shifted gears to devote all his efforts to become an expert in wine and fine distilled spirits.

Reid Mitenbuler is the author of *Bourbon Empire: The Past and Future of America's Whiskey*. He has written about spirits for *The Atlantic, Whisky Advocate, The Daily Beast,* and *Slate,* among other publications.

Liza Weisstuch is the American contributing editor to *Whisky Magazine*. Her work has appeared in the *New York Times*, the *Washington Post*, the *Wall Street Journal, Smithsonian Magazine, Whisky Advocate, The Daily Beast,* and the *Boston Globe*. She has developed her well-rounded spirits education by visiting more than 130 distilleries in seventeen countries.

Index

Colophon

The text and heads of this book is set in *Franklin ITC Pro*, designed in 2007 by David Berlow.

It was printed and bound in South Korea by Pacom Korea, Inc.

It was indexed by Elizabeth T. Parson.

The cover and end papers were designed by Phaedra Charles.

It was edited by Susannah Skiver Barton and George Scott.